BILLY GRAHAM:
LEADING
WITH LOVE

BILLY GRAHAM: LEADING WITH LOVE

5 Timeless Principles for Effective Leaders

Matt Woodley, General Editor

Waterfall
PRESS

Portions of this book originally published under the title *Leadership
Secrets of Billy Graham* with original authorship, interviews, and
research work by Harold Myra, Marshall Shelley, and Collin
Hanson. Editorial work for this book by Bonnie McMaken and
Kevin Emmert under the direction of Matt Woodley.

ISBN-13: 9781477823583
ISBN-10: 1477823581

Cover Design by Laura Klynstra

Library of Congress Control Number: 2014930872

Printed in the United States of America

First printing—May 2014

TABLE OF CONTENTS

INTRODUCTION

When you hear the name Billy Graham, do you think first of his leadership? Most of us do not. Instead, for millions of Americans, the name Billy Graham is primarily associated with speaking at mass evangelistic meetings, calling people to faith in Christ. Yet Billy begins his autobiography by saying, "My responsibilities as chief executive officer of the Billy Graham Association have always demanded a tremendous amount of time and decision making." For over six decades, Billy was a powerful preacher and evangelist, but his track record also reveals that he was a leader of leaders, a spiritual father figure who acted with courage and conviction, and a man who led a large and complex organization that has significantly impacted history. Thousands of effective leaders across the globe still credit Billy for igniting their own leadership and commitment to Christian ministry.

How did he become this visionary chief executive with such a strong entrepreneurial force, engaging millions of individuals and at the same time helping to build strong, burgeoning institutions? Billy himself would say he was simply the instrument God chose to use.

Harold Myra, the former president of the organization that Billy founded, Christianity Today, had a unique opportunity to see Graham's leadership skills in action. Myra wrote:

> [Shortly after joining Christianity Today], I began to understand that Billy was not only CEO of the Billy Graham Evangelistic

Association but also powerfully influenced many institutions [including Young Life, Youth for Christ, InterVarsity, Wheaton College, Fuller and Gordon-Conwell Seminaries, World Relief, World Vision, and the Salvation Army]. He encouraged, counseled, prodded, and cast the broad vision. After observing Billy at one CT board meeting, I thought, *He not only does all the things we see on TV and read about in the press, but behind the scenes he's inspiring the leadership of an entire movement.*

In a personal letter to Myra, Billy was much more modest.

"It seems to me," he wrote, "the Lord took several inexperienced young men and used them in ways we never dreamed. The ministry sort of took off and got away from all of us! We all seemed to be a part of a tremendous movement of the Spirit of God, and so many of the new organizations seemed to interrelate, or began as we talked and prayed together on our travels."

Although hundreds of books and thousands of articles have been written about Billy Graham, his role as an executive leader has been largely unexplored. The discovery process for this book was initiated by Harold Myra, along with Marshall Shelley, the current editor in chief at *Leadership Journal.* These two journalists, assisted by Collin Hanson, started interviewing Billy's closest associates, the highly accomplished leaders who labored beside him for decades. They wanted to know what it was like to have Billy as a boss and a team captain. They also scoured through written materials by and about Billy—books, biographies, original letters, and other resources. They reflected on that which challenged, energized, and sustained him throughout his ministry. Billy not only drew from the Bible, which he constantly quoted, he also drew from the rich traditions of Christian scholars and theologians.

Myra and Shelley selected and sorted through the plethora of resources about Billy while also interviewing key players in Billy's life. They began this process with plenty of questions. For instance, how did Billy have such a reputation for humility and yet be so much in the spotlight, meeting with the world's most powerful leaders and receiving some of the nation's most distinguished honors? Why did the press seek him out so frequently? He used leadership principles from some of the most famous leadership experts, and yet he probably read few, if any, of those books. Where did his skills come from? And how could he endure harsh and even brutal criticism year after year, along with deep and devastating betrayal, and yet maintain his optimism?

This book explores Billy Graham's role as a leader by analyzing five aspects of leadership common to almost any leader in any organization. Part One focuses on how Billy reflected the *character* of a leader. Part Two looks at Billy and his team's commitment to the *mission* of their organization. Part Three addresses the importance of *teamwork* and how Billy built and sustained a team that stayed unified and intact over the years. Part Four walks through some of the most common *challenges* faced by leaders. Part Five explores how *faith* in God shaped and nurtured Billy's life as a leader.

The mosaic that emerges from Billy's leadership is rich, complex, and utterly human. This book is not intended to lionize Billy Graham. After all, Billy himself often admitted his need for ongoing growth as a leader and as a follower of Christ. And yet this book is unapologetically positive because of its purpose—to provide an inspirational and practical example for other leaders.

Billy always insisted on simply being called "Billy." He titled his autobiography *Just As I Am*, a perfect description of his humble spirit, taken from the hymn sung while he invited people to come forward and receive God's love. With humble audacity and ferocious resolve, Billy led with a full awareness of his strengths and weaknesses.

Those of us called to some sort of leadership realize that "just as I am" describes each of us as we face demanding, complex challenges. In the refining furnace of leadership, we sense we must seek empowerment from above. And we know we simply must do the best we can with what we have and who we are.

Billy Graham did that. Whatever the challenges and hurdles, whatever the limitations, he steadily led by a full commitment to biblical values. His lifetime of vigorous leadership invites every leader to engage with the same spirit, to consider his example, and to dig, as he did, into the rich resources of leadership literature that resonate with biblical principles.

PART ONE
CHARACTER

The word *character* derived from a word that was used in connection with tools for engraving or branding. Thus, a person's character "marked" him or her. By the mid-1600s, character referred to the sum total of a person's qualities. In other words, your character is the *real* you. It's who you are when no one is looking.

Throughout his long and very public ministry, Billy Graham was marked by a consistent, predictable, and Christlike character. The sum of Billy's qualities remained the same whether he was with presidents, popes, or handymen; whether he was in the spotlight in front of thousands or alone in his hotel room; whether his popularity was soaring or his critics were hounding him. This section focuses on three leadership qualities that marked Graham's life: his *integrity* in the face of temptation, his *humility* in the face of egoism, and his *courage* in the face of tough decisions.

For Graham, growing in character as a leader wasn't a self-improvement project. Nor was Graham's character an attempt to earn God's favor and impress other people. Instead, Graham's virtues were always a response to God's grace. As Graham himself said in the introduction to his autobiography, "Most of all, if anything has been accomplished through my life, it has been solely God's doing, not mine, and he—not I—must get the credit."

CHAPTER 1
CONFRONTING TEMPTATION

Biographer William Martin tells the story of George Bergin, a rough-hewn handyman who acted as the caretaker for the Graham's home in Montreat, North Carolina. After Martin spent some time interviewing Billy and Ruth, Bergin gave Martin a ride along a steep and narrow mountain road. Bergin turned to Martin and said, "You've been visiting some mighty good people today. My wife and I have been knowing Mister and Miz Graham for fifteen years, and I'm telling you, they're the same inside the house as out."[i]

The Grahams' neighbor and handyman identified a major trait of Billy's leadership—his *integrity*. Throughout six decades of public ministry, many people from all walks of life hailed Billy as a leader of uncommon character. Even his harshest critics couldn't tarnish Graham's integrity. But it wasn't because Billy didn't have opportunities to succumb to temptation. During the height of his popularity, political and spiritual leaders from around the globe sought his advice. Every year millions of people would show up to hear him preach. Journalists, celebrities, and athletes wanted to be with him. At one point 90 percent of the people in Great Britain recognized Graham's name. Every year the Graham organization took in millions of dollars. As former *Christianity Today* magazine editor V. Gilbert Beers once noted, "This is the stuff of which corruption is made."

From the start of his ministry, Graham was surrounded by the common temptations that have tripped up numerous leaders—power, fame, sex, and money. As he became more influential and more visible in the public eye, the scope of these temptations only grew for Billy and his team. And yet, nearly everyone agrees that there's one word that sums up Billy's character—integrity. Longtime friend and colleague John Stott once said, "If I had to choose one word with which to characterize Billy Graham, it would be integrity. He was all of a piece. There was no dichotomy between what he said and who he was. He practiced what he preached."

So how did Billy combat temptation without being legalistic? What were the commitments he was unwilling to bend on, and how did he protect these through discipline and accountability?

The Radical Manifesto

Billy Graham was well known for his ministry partnerships with people like George Beverly Shea, Cliff Barrows, and others. But early in his ministry, before he became a household name for his Crusades, Billy worked as a field representative for Youth for Christ, traveling extensively to speak to various groups, churches, and colleges. In fact, in 1945 alone he visited forty-seven states.

During all this travel, he met many evangelists who had faced and capitulated to various temptations. Historian George Marsden said, "[When Billy saw] the terrible disillusionment trusting church folks had suffered [from the double lives of these evangelists] ... it added an increasingly dogged determination to adhere to high standards of morality and ethics."

In November 1948, Billy would have the chance to define and express the baseline convictions for his life and for his ministry. But he wouldn't do it alone. By this time, he had formed a small evangelistic team of several other gifted Christians he trusted. This entire team, which was meeting in Modesto, California, was particularly grieved by the moral failings of other pastors and evangelists, many of who were colleagues in Christ or personal friends.

Billy told his team, "God has brought us to this point. Maybe he is preparing us for something that we don't know. Let's try to recall all the things that have been a stumbling block and a hindrance to evangelists in years past, and let's come back together in an hour and talk about it and pray about it and ask God to guard us from them."

So the team members went to their separate hotel rooms and made their own lists of specific areas of temptation and how they would handle those temptations. When they came back together, their lists were surprisingly similar. Then they finalized a single list for the entire organization, put it in writing, and vowed before God and each other that they would uphold one another in these areas. This historic and ministry-defining list came to be known as the "Modesto Manifesto."

For the Graham team, the Modesto Manifesto put clearly on the table the issue of temptations. Ever after, the subject was no longer taboo but one that could be openly addressed. But the Graham team also recognized the need to put the right reinforcements into the structure of their work.

Billy recalls, "In reality, it did not mark a radical departure for us; we had always held these principles. It did, however, settle in our hearts and minds, once and for all, the determination that integrity would be the hallmark of both our lives and our ministry." Clearly, Billy surrounded himself with godly leaders who were willing not only to live exemplary lives but also uphold him as he strived to do the same.

Integrity Listens

Often, when a leader becomes more successful and influential, others are afraid to offer their feedback. Sometimes the leader compounds that fear by acting unapproachable and defensive. But Billy was so committed to team-wide transparency that he accepted and even *requested* feedback and accountability from those he trusted.

Bill Pollard, former CEO of ServiceMaster and a BGEA board member, explained: "He has strong convictions and views about many things. But at the same time, he demonstrates his genuine desire to serve under the authority of those who will keep him from stumbling."

Because Billy's board was composed of people he knew and trusted, he frequently asked for their thoughts on a number of issues, creating a dialogue and a greater level of trust within the team. This started with the Modesto Manifesto and grew even stronger over the years. V. Gilbert Beers said, "Graham held himself accountable to his associates. We all need strong friends who will lovingly slam doors in our faces ... Integrity listens when wise friends say 'no.'"

The Power of Greed

When Billy and his team started the Crusades, they took love offerings to sustain their ministry. Obviously, administrating a vast nonprofit organization required plenty of money. Billy and his team mentioned this as a primary temptation when they created the Modesto Manifesto. And they knew that they weren't exempt from the power of greed.

Billy recalls, "The temptation to wring as much money as possible out of an audience, often with strong emotional appeals, was too great for some evangelists. In addition, there was little or no accountability for finances. In Modesto we determined to do all we could to avoid financial abuses and to downplay the offering and depend as much as possible on money raised by the local committees in advance."

Part of this transparency meant installing a series of checks and balances regarding the use of funds, which ensured that even if the temptation to greed arose, Billy couldn't take advantage of the love offerings the ministry received at crusades. For example, Billy's team asked a sponsoring committee to oversee paying the bills and disbursing funds to the revival team.

It was this kind of financial stewardship that marked Billy's ministry, even when it affected him personally. Bill Pollard recalls a story about Billy having to travel to Europe in early summer, flying back to the States, and then going back to Hungary for meetings in August. At the time, his health was poor, so, as Pollard recalls, "Billy came to the board and said, 'Between the time the first commitment in Europe ends and the beginning of the Hungary campaign the second week of August, I'd like to ask your permission to stay in Europe to prepare for the meetings and avoid the jetlag back and forth.'"

This openness had a deep impact on Billy's board. Pollard recalls, "I was impressed that he wouldn't even spend the money for something like that without board approval. That's just an example of the way he has conducted himself in submission to authority."

Silo-free Living

Business leader Patrick Lencioni identified a prominent symptom of corporate frustration: silos, which he defines as "the invisible barriers that separate [teams], causing people who are supposed to be on the same team to work against one another."[ii] According to Lencioni, silos—and the turf wars they enable—devastate organizations by wasting resources, killing productivity, and jeopardizing results. This silo effect leaves leaders more vulnerable to the subtle temptations that function like blind spots in the rearview mirror.

In contrast, Billy Graham consistently tried to avoid silo-type leadership by collaborating with others. The ministry could have easily become like a circus: pull into a town, set up the tent, put on a show, tear it all down, and leave. No commitments, no ties to anything or anyone in the local community, including the local church.

But this wasn't the way Billy and his team practiced ministry. He said:

> We had observed the tendency of many evangelists to carry on their work apart from the local church, even to criticize local pastors and churches openly and scathingly. We were convinced, however, that this was not only counterproductive but also wrong from the Bible's standpoint. We were determined to cooperate with all who would cooperate with us in the public proclamation of the gospel, and to avoid an anti-church or anti-clergy attitude.

Notice the key line that seemed to define Graham's leadership in this area: "We were determined to cooperate with all who would cooperate with us..."

Billy even developed friendships with non-Christians, although there were those who criticized his connections with certain politicians and celebrities. From time to time, he shared a stage with these public figures and met with them to discuss how to deal with troubling pervasive social issues. But Graham's mission focus enabled him to view these partnerships as opportunities to share the gospel.

Publicity Integrity

Early in his ministry, Billy noted a troubling trend among his fellow evangelists. He labeled it the tendency "to exaggerate or to claim higher attendance numbers than they really had." Billy wrote, "This likewise discredited evangelism and brought the whole enterprise under suspicion. It often made the press so suspicious of evangelists that they refused to take notice of their work. In Modesto we committed ourselves to integrity in our publicity and our reporting."

Leighton Ford, one of Graham's longtime associates, remembers a breakfast meeting with pastors during one campaign, years after Modesto. The campaign committee was reporting an inaccuracy. "Gardner Taylor spoke up," Leighton recalls. "He said, 'Dr. Graham, I think we must always say just what is the truth.' Billy immediately agreed. He always insisted on total integrity."

A big part of this integrity for Billy's ministry was transparency about the numbers of people at the crusades and other events, where it would have been easy to inflate the numbers. The Graham team decided to accept the crowd size estimates provided by local police or other officials, even when the team felt the estimates were too low.

Graham's team called those who came forward after a sermon "inquirers" rather than converts. After all, no one can know what actually happens inside a person's soul, and the Graham team chose not to presumptuously tally spiritual transactions. It was another way of fighting the temptation to exaggerate their accomplishments.

This commitment helped Billy deal with the lure of success. As David Aikman, the former *Time* magazine correspondent said, "The test of Graham's soul, indeed, lay not in adversity, but in how he coped with success."

Sexual Integrity

The reality of sexual temptation became one of the motivating factors behind the Modesto Manifesto. It was a stumbling block for many evangelists who tasted power and fame. "We all knew of evangelists who had fallen into immorality while separated from their families by travel," Billy wrote. "We pledged among ourselves to avoid any situation that would have even the appearance of compromise or suspicion. From that day on, I did not travel, meet, or eat alone with a woman other than my wife. We determined that the apostle Paul's mandate to the young pastor Timothy would be ours as well: 'Flee... youthful lusts' (2 Timothy 2:22, KJV)." Billy and his team went beyond just avoiding a moral fall; they wanted to eliminate any *suspicion* of impropriety. Billy said, "[We asked God] to guard us, to keep us true, to really help us be sensitive in this area and keep us even from the appearance of evil."

But Billy wasn't ashamed of human sexuality. During a crusade in Berlin, a young female correspondent for Germany's largest mass-circulation magazine, *Der Spiegel*, cornered him and asked, "Mr. Graham, what do you think about sex?" Billy replied, "Sex is the most wonderful thing on this earth... as long as God is in it. When the devil gets in it, it's the most terrible thing on this earth."[iii]

Billy's guidelines for sexual integrity had an impact on other leaders around him. Media management consultant David Schmidt said that the example of Billy Graham and his associates helped him resist the inevitable temptations of travel. "You get tempted in hotel rooms to put something on TV you shouldn't. I knew the stories of how Billy would never be alone with a woman—how he was very careful about all this stuff—and the men around him were careful, too. They weren't hiding things; they worked at personal purity. They'd say, 'You have to be in the dark what you are in the light!' That helped me to aim for a higher standard."

Only One Billy Graham

V. Gilbert Beers remembers a simple story that typifies the character that marked Billy Graham's life. In 1984 Beers visited Graham in Liverpool to interview him after a closing crusade. During an interview over dinner, Beers recalls that Billy was like a celebrity and many people called to him from the street. But Billy was unaffected. He could have taken a limo to a fancy restaurant, but instead he took a simple car to a casual restaurant.

Beers offered the following assessment of Graham's character:

> The man sitting there eating hamburgers and fries with us was just an ordinary guy. That's not profound, but it is profound that forty years of worldwide public attention have not convinced him otherwise. People have shouted at him from every corner that he is a great man; but he's stone deaf. He just doesn't hear what they're saying.
>
> It is easy to identify a person of integrity, but it is not so easy to pinpoint what makes him so. Billy Graham ... and his associates have determined that he will live beyond reproach. It's not merely a creed, but a commitment. Graham lived privately what he preaches publicly. He is consistent. What he believes, says, and does are the same. There is only one Billy Graham, not a public one and a private one.

CHAPTER 2
REDEEMING THE EGO

Nik Wallenda has become the most-watched high-wire artist and daredevil in the world. His two most recent feats—a tightrope walk across the Niagara Falls (2012) and a high-wire walk across the Grand Canyon (2013)—were seen by a billion people worldwide. Wallenda, a committed Christian, worries about pride, so after the huge crowds and the media fade away, he engages in a simple spiritual discipline: he walks where the crowds have just stood and picks up trash. Wallenda offers the following explanation:

> My purpose is simply to help clean up after myself. Huge crowds leave a great deal of trash behind, and I feel compelled to pitch in. Besides, after the inordinate amount of attention I sought and received ... three hours of cleaning up debris is good for my soul. Humility does not come naturally to me. So if I have to force myself into situations that are humbling, so be it.... As a follower of Jesus, I see him washing the feet of others. I do it because if I don't serve others I'll be serving nothing but my ego.[iv]

Wallenda highlights a major issue for many leaders: the power of the ego. At times it's as starkly real as serving others or serving your ego. Billy Graham's global influence with powerful people could have made him utterly egotistical. Instead, somehow Billy found a way to navigate around the vortex of personal ego.

On one occasion, Bill Mead, Graham's first executive commit-tee chair, joined Billy on a trip to see President Lyndon Johnson at his ranch home. Johnson was terminally ill, so the conversation focused on Johnson's funeral plans. Mead recalls, "Johnson was sit-ting on the front porch with his dog on his lap, and then we rode around in his convertible. Lyndon would tell Billy what he wanted done at his funeral. Two weeks after that, Johnson died. He had felt Billy was from God himself."

Mead uses this story to highlight two leadership qualities that marked Billy's life—"presence" and humility. Graham's personal presence commanded respect from presidents, and yet his ego stayed in check. Someone once asked business leader Fred Smith how Billy could be so humble and handle his ego while enjoy-ing the company of presidents. "The ego must be redeemed," Fred replied. "And you can tell when someone allows God to redeem his ego. I was chair of Billy's Cincinnati campaign and was with him at a breakfast with a reporter who was critical of Billy. He asked him some hard questions. However, the published story turned out positive. Billy then told me, with a grin, 'Fred, they don't care if you're a nut so long as you're a sincere nut.' He didn't take himself too seriously."

The word *ego* has at least two definitions: 1) "a regarding of one's self with undue favor" (synonymous with *conceit* or *vanity*) and 2) "a sense of one's own dignity or worth" (synonymous with *self-respect*). "Redeeming the ego" implies orienting your life around the second definition rather than the first. It requires humility and meekness. Smith put it this way: "Humility is not denying the power you have. It is realizing that the power comes through you, not from you."

The poet Mary Karr once captured the Bible's view of meek-ness by picturing a great stallion at full gallop. At his master's voice, he "seizes up to a stunned but instant halt." Karr then eloquently describes the stallion holding its "great power" in check, listening for the next order. In the same way, Billy's presence exuded influence, but like a great stallion, when Billy heard his Master's voice. He listened and at times "seized up to a stunned but instant halt."

A parallel image is Billy, the humble farm boy from rural America, totally awed by all that happened to him. Time and again he expressed total wonder at what has been done through him. He is the boy-become-man who sees far more clearly than most of the mixed motives of human souls.

Sheer Amazement

The mix of Mead's words to describe Billy—*presence, respect,* and *humility*—seem oddly juxtaposed. Having the charisma to command respect at the highest levels and the ability to turn hostile reporters into advocates would naturally inflate anyone's ego. Yet many colleagues and friends testified to Billy's humility. Lon Allison, former director of the Billy Graham Center at Wheaton College, said, "You simply don't have the sense you're with this world-famous person. If you hear him talk, he always uses the plural pronoun—never *I*." He tells the story of when he first met Billy:

[A colleague] introduced us saying, "You know, Bill, Lon did his doctoral research in evangelistic preaching and communications." Billy put his hand on my shoulder and said with all seriousness, "Maybe you could teach me a few things." I just burst out laughing. It was totally unexpected. I said something like, "Well, since most of my work is based on your life, I doubt it." But Billy was totally serious.

One of President Lyndon Johnson's biographers noted that his Texas-sized ego prompted him to refer even to his cabinet members by the first-person possessive: "I'd like you to meet *my* secretary of state," he'd say, as if the United States government was peopled by his own personal lackeys. In contrast, Billy realized that his success was never the result of his own work. The ministry wasn't his; it was God's.

This God-centered view of his gifts and success started early in his ministry. After his 1949 Los Angeles crusade, Billy was stunned by the results. As usual, his wife Ruth shared his amazement. "We felt we were just spectators," she said. "God was doing something, and Billy and I were just watching." On November 21, when the crusade finally ended and their train was pulling out of the Los Angeles station, both husband and wife humbly sank to their knees in gratitude, praise, and awe.

Just Another Sinner

As mentioned in the introduction, Billy titled his autobiography *Just As I Am,* the title of the hymn sung during his invitations to receive Christ. In choosing that title for his own life story, Billy identified himself with every inquirer walking to the front and confessing sin and weakness. He was stating that he stands in line with every other sinner and convert, getting ready to receive God's grace. Although Billy was a world-class evangelist who spent night after night in front of hundreds of thousands of people, he didn't like drawing attention to himself. Graeme Keith, treasurer of the BGEA and a lifelong friend, once said, "I was on an elevator with Billy when another man in the elevator recognized him. He said, 'You're Billy Graham, aren't you?'

"'Yes,' Billy said.

"'Well,' he said, 'you are truly a great man.'

"Billy immediately responded, 'No, I'm not a great man. I just have a great message.'"

When Billy deflected the glory away from himself, it wasn't a case of false humility. He really did connect his success back to God's grace, not his own effort and ingenuity.

Billy's grandson, Pastor Tullian Tchividjian, said:

Daddy Bill was always keenly aware that God was God and he was not. He was conscious of his smallness and God's bigness, his imperfection and God's perfection. Not long ago, I told someone that it wasn't until I got older that I realized how well-known and significant my grandfather was. This was mainly due to the fact that he never, ever, projected himself to be more or less important than anyone else. I didn't think he was extraordinary because *he* didn't think he was extraordinary. I never once saw him "think more highly of himself than he ought."

Billy has always been aware of his own shortcomings. He openly admitted struggling with his inadequacy for the task that was placed on his shoulders. That's one reason why it was often painful for him to hear long, adulatory introductions. He felt truly humble laboring under the magnificence of God. In fact, his feelings about his alleged "greatness" could create a strong reaction from Billy. In the groundbreaking ceremonies for his new headquarters, quoting the words of John the Baptist, Billy said, "Jesus must increase, and I must decrease. I cringe when I hear my name called in something that has been the work of God through these years."

Just One of Many Factors

In a David Frost interview, Billy said that, when he preached, "the Holy Spirit is the communicating agent.... People are really not listening to me.... They're listening to another voice inside, the voice of the Holy Spirit." Billy went on to tell Frost that even when he might have preached the message poorly and left out things he wanted to say, "God knows my motive and he knows my heart, and God uses even that simple presentation that might have been poorly done, and he applies it to the human heart."

Elsewhere, Billy said, "I never claim that I lead anybody to Christ. I am just one in a series of many factors that bring people to this giving of themselves to the Savior." Billy grasped the vast gulf between human imperfection and God's magnificence, between human limitations and God's power.

But for Billy this theological perspective didn't produce passivity; instead, it energized and focused Billy's ministry efforts. In a 1984 conversation at the Billy Graham Center, Billy told a colleague, "God's given me one great gift. I have a gift of bringing people to Christ. And that I've got to do." During a June 2005 interview, Larry King asked Billy how he wanted to be remembered. With his characteristic humility, Billy simply said, "That he was faithful to the gospel." On another occasion, Billy expressed a similar combination of humility and passion. "I intend to keep on going," he said, "preaching the gospel, writing the gospel, as long as I have any breath. I hope my last word as I am dying… I hope my dying word will be Jesus."[v]

But his perceived failures didn't keep him from moving forward; rather, they energized him all the more. The Christian tradition has often viewed failure and humiliation as a deepening and purifying process.

The Ego Trap

Billy thought large but lived small. He preached at hundreds of crusades, established the BGEA, launched a radio program, founded two magazines, and started a film company and several other organizations. But he strove to keep his ego in check, because he knew he couldn't work alone and realized that he needed God's help. In short, Billy saw himself as a simple workman with a huge mandate.

Billy was troubled by the trap of egotism. "I feel that people have put me on too high a pedestal," he said in a *New York Times* column. "We do the same with other leaders," Billy explained. "I know, however, that I am not as good as some people think I am. I have seen men in the depths of wickedness, and I have thought to myself, 'There I go, except by the grace of God.'"

Billy's fear of the "ego trap" compelled him to be brutally honest about his own limitations. As an example, in a David Frost interview Billy freely admitted that he often felt like he had failed at preaching. Frost asked, "So there can never be a feeling that 'I've done badly; I've failed tonight'?" Billy responded, "Oh, I have that feeling quite often. In fact, most of the time I wish that I could have represented the gospel better. Really, that's a sincere feeling. Almost every night I say, 'I wish I had done better,' because I'm a representative, really, of Christ. That's a tremendous responsibility."

The Power of Humility

As demonstrated in Billy's life, humility isn't just a private virtue; instead, it spills over into communal life. During a meeting in Mexico City for Christian leaders from around the globe, a controversy arose regarding how to balance two valid biblical activities—evangelism and social action. All the evangelical leaders who were present agreed that both were important, but a controversy arose about how to put the two activities into practice. Even longtime friends Billy Graham and John Stott found themselves on different sides of the debate. But Graham displayed his leadership by acting with humility and openness to the "other side" of the controversy.

William Martin describes the impact of Graham's humility:

The effect was extraordinary. One observer recalled that, "as [Graham] began to open his heart, sharing with us his deep personal feelings, I never witnessed a more magnanimous expression of tenderness and understanding. His insight to the situation, his sensitivity to personalities, amplified by his humility, literally melted us."

Another member of the committee said:

[On seeing] his humility, the graciousness of his spirit, and his genuine desire to be open to the Lord and to the counsel of the Lord's people, I became convinced that Dr. Graham actually felt that he had much yet to learn and that he needed the counsel and help of other Christians. For a man in his position actually to reflect that kind of attitude is to me remarkable and a great challenge.[vi]

As evidenced in Billy's life, true Christlike humility is powerful. It melts hearts. It builds bridges of friendship. It forges Christian community.

No wonder C.S. Lewis could write, "To even get near [humility], even for a moment, is like a drink of cold water to a man in a desert." If you met a truly humble person, Lewis said, "Probably all you will think about him is that he seemed a cheerful, intelligent chap who took a real interest in what *you* said to *him*." Lewis said that you might feel a little envious of this humble "chap" because he "seems to enjoy life so easily." Lewis concluded, "He will not be thinking about humility; he will not be thinking about himself at all."[vii]

That captures the essence, the power, and the beauty of Graham's truly humble spirit.

CHAPTER 3
SUMMONING COURAGE

In an interview with *Harvard Business Review*, poet Maya Angelou explained how leaders develop courage. Angelou said she learned from her mother that we aren't born with courage; instead, we develop courage. Angelou explained:

> And you develop it by doing small, courageous things, in the same way that one wouldn't set out to pick up a 100-pound bag of rice. If that was one's aim, the person would be advised to pick up a five-pound bag, and then a ten-pound, and then a twenty-pound, and so forth, until one builds up enough muscle to actually pick up 100 pounds. And that's the same way with courage.
>
> You develop courage by doing courageous things, small things, but things that cost you some exertion—mental and, I suppose, spiritual exertion.[viii]

Angelou's advice certainly resonates with the lifelong leadership lessons of Billy Graham. Throughout his life Billy made decisions that kept him growing in the virtue of courage. As a highly visible leader, every statement and off-the-cuff comment was evaluated, assessed, and analyzed. He often found himself the target of criticism from the press and even from church leaders.

All through the decades of his ministry, he lived with the constant awareness that at any time he could get gunned down by an assassin. He often received hate mail. The FBI and police informed him about numerous death threats. He was always in the public eye, knowing that at any moment someone could take a shot at him—just as someone shot John and Bobby Kennedy, Martin Luther King Jr., John Lennon, and Ronald Reagan.

On one occasion, a man called Billy at his hotel and warned, "Mr. Graham, some of us are going to kill you before midnight tonight." On another occasion early in his ministry, he was leading a service when, in the middle of it, he was told a pastor had called to warn him a man was coming to murder him. Billy told the audience about it but continued with the service.

Death threats, hate mail, dialogue with hostile intellectuals or cynical reporters, critics on the left and the right, the ire of ecclesiastical critics and self-appointed "heresy-hunters"—at nearly every step along his ministry Graham had to choose to pick up a ten-, twenty-, or thirty-pound weight of courage. At times, on major initiatives he diligently and with great thoroughness sought wisdom and counsel before devoting his full energies to implementing a plan of action—only to see his efforts assaulted. Naturally, at times he got discouraged, but throughout his ministry Billy also displayed a consistent pattern of living courageously. This chapter explores what true courage looks like as displayed in Billy's character.

Start with Surrender

For Billy, courage never came from sheer heroic, human strength or the force of will-power. Instead, his life demonstrated a biblical principle: True courage is a by-product of trusting God and surrendering our fears to him on a daily basis. His wife Ruth once expressed this truth when she said that true peace and courage comes from believing that "nothing can touch a child of God without his permission."ix

One of the most profound displays of Billy's courageous leadership occurred on his historic trip to Communist Russia in 1982. None of his trips were as fraught with complexity and controversy—before, during, and after the trip. Billy had numerous chances to ditch his convictions and run away from the opportunity. But he stuck to his convictions, took the trip to Russia, and then defended his actions.

What sustained Billy as he faced the onslaught of objections and criticisms about his decision to preach in Russia? It was primarily his consistent surrender to God and God's mission for his life. Graham's vision for ministry in the Soviet Union had begun long before 1982. In 1959, though unable to get permission to hold meetings there, he visited the Soviet Union as a tourist. Sitting with friend and ministry partner Grady Wilson, Billy gazed across the vast expanse of an empty Lenin Stadium in Moscow. The great coliseum, site of Soviet athletic triumphs and numerous Communist Party celebrations, felt strangely impotent without the throngs of Russian spectators. He envisioned standing before those masses, preaching the good news of Christ in a country where God had been outlawed. Communist officials had barred him from speaking publicly, so instead Billy simply bowed his head and prayed that God would one day bring him back to the Soviet capital and allow him to share the gospel.

"And yet for decades, it seemed as if that was one prayer God would never answer, an unrealistic pipe dream that could never come true," Billy wrote in his autobiography. "The barriers were too great, the wall erected by Communism against religion too impregnable."

After years of waiting and probing, Billy's prayer was answered—he returned to Russia as an evangelistic preacher. But notice that Billy's courageous decision and his tenacity to keep pursuing that decision didn't start with will-power; it started and was sustained with prayer and surrender.

Here's how Sherwood Wirt, Billy's longtime friend and the first editor for Graham's *Decision* magazine, described the power source for Billy's convictions and character:

> Here is the secret: Billy Graham is filled with the Spirit of God. That is the source of his inner power. His life is not so much controlled as invaded by this unseen Source. No matter where he is, no matter what the situation might be in which he finds himself, no matter what his physical condition, he is never more than a half second out of touch with God.[x]

Face Complexity

Acting courageously doesn't always mean that issues are clear and simple. In other words, courage doesn't take place in the absence of doubts. The facts don't always line up. The picture isn't always clear. At times leaders need to step out in faith and courage even in the face of uncertainty and complexity—which is exactly what Billy had to do in his 1982 trip to Russia.

Eventually, after long and complex negotiations, Communist authorities gave a green light, with some conditions. Billy would not be permitted to preach in any of Russia's great stadiums, as he had prayed in 1959, but he would be able to speak in both Baptist and Orthodox churches. There was just one catch: He would also be expected to participate in a gathering called "The World Conference of Religious Workers for Saving the Sacred Gift of Life from Nuclear Catastrophe." That was a problem. Despite the noble-sounding purpose and religious sponsorship, such meetings were infamous for being Communist-manipulated, anti-American propaganda events. How could he participate and give his implied endorsement to such a farce? The Reagan administration and his conservative supporters back home would surely be opposed.

Billy agonized over the decision. Two years before, the United States had boycotted the Summer Olympics in Moscow to protest the Soviet invasion of Afghanistan. President Ronald Reagan had delivered hard-line addresses and would soon use the "Evil Empire" phrase to describe the Soviet system. Would Billy be undermining his country?

When Billy asked the advice of Allan Emery and George Bennett, two of his trusted board members, they counseled him not to go. They feared that the risk to his reputation would be too great if the Soviets used him for political gain. In contrast, Dr. Alexander Haraszti, a Hungarian Christian leader, adamantly said he should go, arguing, "The Lord has opened the door, and we must enter the door." Haraszti pointed out that if Billy's reputation suffered, it wouldn't compare to the sufferings of Russian Christians. He urged Billy to take the long view: "You must not jeopardize the ten years to come. This is the beginning…. This will be your first coming to the Soviet Union but not your last one. If you accept the invitation, all the other satellite countries will fall in line. These things are interwoven. No Moscow, no satellite countries."

But Billy's friend, Vice President George H. W. Bush, called him to tell him the U.S. ambassador to the Soviet Union did not want him to go. Billy was torn by compelling arguments on both sides.

Finally, in the midst of deep uncertainty that included mixed opinions from trustworthy people on both sides, he decided to accept the invitation. As we'll see, the mission was successful and his decision was eventually vindicated as the right course of action. But Billy didn't know that at the time. He had to surrender to God, trust the Holy Spirit, and then take a risk in light of unclear data. As Martin Luther King Jr. famously said, "Faith is taking the first step even when you can't see the whole staircase." It takes courage to live with that kind of faith.

Relinquish People-Pleasing

Here's one sure dead end for leaders: trying to please everyone all the time. Eventually we'll need the courage to relinquish our compulsion to please others. People-pleasing is a fruitless, exhausting job. The sooner leaders can resign from that job, the more they'll thrive as leaders.

Billy learned this lesson well both during and after his Russia trip. As the trip progressed, public opinion against Billy increased. For instance, when Billy visited the dissident "Siberian Seven" (Pentecostals who had sought asylum in the U.S. embassy, becoming a worldwide symbol for religious freedom), many anti-Communists criticized Billy for not denouncing the Soviet Union on their behalf. Throughout the trip, Billy's comments, meant to be gracious and evenhanded, were interpreted as naive. Back home in the United States, the media were sharply critical.

The Baltimore Sun editorialized, "Billy Graham has a God-given right to make a fool of himself in Moscow. He's doing a pretty good job of it while attending a propaganda show." Political cartoonists depicted Billy abandoning persecuted Christians, many of whom labored in Siberian work camps like Aleksandr Solzhenitsyn before them. Even his hometown newspaper, *The Charlotte Observer,* posed him in a cartoon next to a Soviet-looking Julius Caesar and remarked, "Billy Graham never met a Caesar he didn't like!" The rhetorical firestorm triggered *Christianity Today* to observe, "Never before in all his career has the evangelist faced such condemnation from the American press and from evangelical leaders."

Because he moved on to England after his trip to the Soviet Union, Billy remained largely unaware of the tumult back home. He did not know that fifty protesters had been marching around the Billy Graham Center at Wheaton College carrying signs like "Graham Eats Caviar as Russian Christians Suffer in Jails." Unlike the American commotion, the European press had reacted more favorably to Billy's Russian venture. They applauded his address to the peace conference.

But Billy became acutely aware of the controversy when he agreed to appear via satellite from London on *This Week with David Brinkley*. He was immediately startled by the pointed and confrontational questioning of Brinkley, Sam Donaldson, and George Will. Mark Azbel, a Jewish Soviet dissident, and Edmund Robb, an evangelical Graham ally, joined the tag-team fray to heap on even more criticism.

George Will chided, "What makes you think that you're going to cause the Kremlin to begin dismantling the apparatus of thought control that's the basis of their regime?"

Sam Donaldson joined the fracas by asking, "Why not preach here at home? Aren't there people in the United States who need your ministry? Your critics say your ego requires a worldwide ministry."

Even his evangelical ally Edmund Robb was critical: "We feel like impressions have been made that are unfortunate. I love you, I believe in you, and I shall continue to be your supporter. But I am convinced you've made a serious mistake in your visit to the Soviet Union, and if some of the things you've been quoted as saying are true, they've certainly compromised you with a great deal of the evangelical community."

Graham was caught off-guard, but he defended his calling. "Well, I'll tell you one thing," he said. "I'll continue to preach the gospel whether there are many or few there."

It was a harrowing experience to face so much withering criticism. And in America he learned that the media had isolated the most incendiary and perplexing observations in Moscow, removing them from any context that could have explained them. Soon after returning from his trip, Billy traveled to Chicago to chair a Christianity Today board meeting. He looked exhausted and discouraged. At the meeting, he shared with the trustees a report by journalist Ed Plowman, which put the statements and events in Russia in context. Still, everyone was acutely aware that the American media continued to be hostile. But Billy weathered the emotional hits and stayed the course. His decision to go to the Soviet Union had been carefully considered and prayerfully discerned, and it didn't make any sense to backtrack now.

Trust God for the Results

Ultimately, Billy was vindicated for his historic 1982 trip, but he couldn't know that as the controversy swirled around him. He had to simply keep moving forward and accept the harsh realities of the assaults. For Billy, the only critic who really counted was God. Billy remained certain that God had wanted him to preach in the Soviet Union. He was anything but naive about the trip; he knew Soviet leadership would exact temporary gain from his presence there. "Of course they are using us," he said, "but we are using them as well, and my message is stronger than theirs."

History proved Billy correct. No one can definitively gauge the degree to which Billy Graham contributed to the Iron Curtain's demise. However, in 1990 President George H.W. Bush praised Billy's prescience:

You know, eight years ago, one of the Lord's great ambassadors, Reverend Billy Graham, went to Eastern Europe and the Soviet

Union and, upon returning, spoke of a movement there toward more religious freedom. And perhaps he saw it before many of us, because it takes a man of God to sense the early movement of the hand of God. And yet, who could predict that in 1989 freedom's tide would be economic, political and intellectual or that the walls of bayonets and barbed wire, the walls of tyranny, would come tumbling down.

Dan Rather of CBS, who had joined in the chorus of criticism, later acknowledged that Billy alone had looked past the atheistic Soviet propaganda to see a nation eager for change. Rather said:

> Before anybody else I knew of, and more consistently than anyone else I have known, of any nationality, race, or religion, Reverend Graham was saying, "Spirituality is alive in the Marxist-Leninist-Stalinist states." … Frankly, there were those years when I thought he was wrong, or that he didn't know what he was talking about. It turns out he was right. And give him credit—he also took the time to go and see for himself.

Just as Billy had hoped, the visit to Moscow opened the door for him to preach without censorship behind the Iron Curtain. He returned to the Soviet Union in 1984 and 1988; he toured Hungary and Romania in 1985; he preached in China in 1988 and North Korea in 1992 and 1994.

In 1992, Billy stood again in Moscow's Olympic Stadium, where he had prayed as a tourist in 1959. Only now, the stadium was not empty. This time Billy shared the message of God's love with 50,000 people crammed in a stadium built for 38,000. Between 20,000 and 30,000 additional people stood outside watching the crusade on projection screens.

Courage Is Contagious

Billy published an article in *Reader's Digest* titled "A Time for Moral Courage."[xi] In it he penned one of his most passionate calls for Christian courage. That short essay contains one of his oft-quoted lines: "Courage is contagious. When a brave man takes a stand, the spines of others are often stiffened." In this same article Billy also wrote the following stirring paragraph:

> The world today, it seems to me, suffers from not only a lack of convictions, but also from timidity in expressing those convictions we do have. Our motto too often seems to be, "Stay aloof. Don't get involved. Let someone else stick his neck out."

Billy concluded the article by calling people not merely to human virtue, but to the saving power of Christ. He wrote:

> The same Simon Peter who cringed before the servant girl's accusations that he was one of Christ's disciples, later became one of those who, the record says, "turned the world upside down." Our world needs turning upside down. Even a small minority can do it, but it takes faith and courage.

Billy didn't just write about the need for courage; he lived a truly courageous life.

PART TWO
MISSION

Every organization needs a clearly defined mission. A mission statement answers fundamental questions like: What do we do? Why do we exist? For example, the mission statement for Nike is "to bring inspiration and innovation to every athlete in the world." The Starbucks website prominently displays their mission: "to inspire and nurture the human spirit—one person, one cup, and one neighborhood at a time." CVS, another Fortune 500 company, has a clear and simple mission: "We will be the easiest pharmacy retailer for customers to use."

Throughout his ministry, Billy Graham led his team and his organization with a clear, biblical, and Christ-centered mission. He focused on spreading the good news of Jesus Christ throughout the globe so others could trust Christ as Lord and Savior. Even to this day, the Billy Graham Evangelistic Association remains focused on that same mission. According to the BGEA website, the organization exists to "proclaim the gospel of the Lord Jesus Christ by every effective means and to equip others to do the same."

Of course, it's not enough to write a mission statement and hang it on a wall. This section explores three aspects of how Billy Graham and his team lived their mission: clarifying and staying focused, birthing new dreams, and raising funds. For six decades of ministry, Billy had an amazing ability to keep his mission front and center.

CHAPTER 4
FOCUSING THE MISSION

Our lives are filled with gadgets we can't use, instructions we can't follow, and forms we can't decipher. Every facet of our lives is complicated by an ever-widening array of choices delivered at a frantic pace. For instance, the average American supermarket carries 48,750 items, more than five times the number of items in 1975.

But according to an article in *The Wall Street Journal,* one company is working hard to counter this complexity trend—the supermarket chain Trader Joe's. This company believes that trying to do too much is a poor business model. It overwhelms customers, clutters stores, and undermines the shopping experience. So Trader Joe's offers fewer products than other supermarkets (about 4,000 items instead of over 48,000). But focusing their mission doesn't lead to ineffectiveness. As a matter of fact, the chain, which has about 350 stores in the United States, sells an estimated $1,750 in merchandise per square foot, more than double the sales generated per square foot by other grocery store chains.[xii]

Why does Trader Joe's business model work? Simply put, they've learned the beauty and power of focusing their mission.

From early on in his ministry, Billy Graham's mission was also laser-focused. He knew who God had created him to be and what God wanted him to pursue. Billy's call to evangelism permeated every aspect of his life, ministry, and public image. Here's how George Brushaber, former president of Bethel University in Minneapolis, described Billy's focus: "There was something about the central passion of his life that attracted his people. Even though many times they were older or had higher education credentials or business success, they held him in awe. There's an anointed, unique quality about him that's hard to describe, a transparency so people could look into his soul. His commitment to his mission was so strong and so clear. The utter simplicity of his agenda is a powerful factor."

The great evangelist of the nineteenth century, Dwight L. Moody, who in many ways was a model for Billy Graham, had a motto: "Consecrate, then concentrate." Billy did just that. He identified his calling and then refused to be diverted. He focused on his mission of evangelism: "to bring people out of their torpor of sin to salvation from it."

To understand Billy's focus, we need to grasp his passion. In his address to the 10,000 international evangelists he brought to Amsterdam in 2000—70 percent who were from the developing world—he said, "The older I get, the more I am asked who will succeed me. Well, the fact is that I am just one of many thousands who have been called to be an evangelist. I don't need a successor, only willing hands to accept the torch I have been carrying."

That "One Thing"

Passionate leaders can easily dabble in a variety of things because they may be good—or even great—at a number of things. Even Billy Graham admits to falling into this trap. "I used to talk on every subject," he admitted. "If somebody asked me anything political, I'd talk on it. I've learned through the years that I'm much better off keeping quiet on certain subjects in order that I may appeal to a wider group of people in my presentation of the gospel."

The danger of trying to focus on everything, however, is that we end up focusing on nothing. Although Billy admits to falling victim to this temptation, he quickly realized that his ministry would be far more effective if he pushed away some of these side issues, many of which were positive, to focus on the one issue that he felt God had laid on his heart: evangelism.

Christian apologist Ravi Zacharias observed, "Billy never changed his calling. Many times it could be said, 'God loved him and *others* had a wonderful plan for his life.' But he kept his focus. Many good things can stand in the way of fulfilling your calling just as much as bad things can. But Billy remained clear on what he was called to."

Billy found that "one thing"—preaching the gospel and bringing people to Christ—and he stuck with it over decades of fruitful ministry.

Rabbits and Stags

Every leader, business, organization, or institution faces a familiar but subtle temptation: the lure of good things, opportunities that *could* consume limited time, energy, and focus. But taking on the wrong projects can render leaders and organizations unable to focus on their true and essential mission. Billy learned not only to pursue his primary God-given calling; he also learned to avoid what he was *not* called to do.

For example, in the mid-1960s Graham and his team were asked to help start a Christian university. Strong voices urged him to consider founding a graduate university, solidly Christian, with academic credentials that would rival Yale or Harvard. But should this be part of Billy's mission? In 1966 he told a reporter, "If someone came along with $10 million to invest in such a school, I'd consider it."

A year later, the conditions were met, and he had to consider it—and make a difficult, and ultimately painful, decision.

The opportunity became a reality when insurance financier John D. MacArthur offered 1,000 acres in Palm Beach Gardens, Florida, along with a pledge of millions of dollars to launch the project. When others heard that Billy would be involved, additional millions of dollars were offered, and planning for Graham University began. But the price for the Graham organization would also be high—approximately $10 million during the first year and $3 million per year for the next five years.

"I consider this a major decision in my life," Billy said, as he wrestled with the pros and cons.

Clearly, Billy was concerned about education. He supported others in their efforts to provide quality Christian education—most notably through the Graham Center at Wheaton College in Illinois and his efforts as a board member to strengthen Gordon-Conwell Divinity School in Massachusetts and Fuller Theological Seminary in California. He placed a high value on the life of the mind.

Ultimately, after long discussions with co-workers and members of his board, he decided the university would divert too much energy and funding away from his primary mission. He backed out of the project, a decision that offended MacArthur and alienated the directors of the foundation that administered his wealth.

At times, maintaining focus is costly, but ultimately the decision enabled Billy to move forward with many major initiatives, including bringing tens of thousands of evangelists together in Amsterdam in 1983, 1986, and 2000, and to put his resources and energies into evangelistic campaigns all over the world.

Jay Kesler, longtime president of Youth for Christ and later president of Taylor University, said, "Billy's great strength is his ability to intuitively go to the center of things. German pastor Helmut Thielicke has written about the difference between the evangelist and the philosopher/teacher/pastor. Thielicke says the evangelist is like a man hunting a [deer]. If you want to hunt stags, you can't shoot at rabbits. If you shoot rabbits, you'll never see a stag. In my mind, Billy Graham was no rabbit shooter. He was always going for the stag."

Billy knew his target. This affected hundreds of small decisions. For instance, in 1970 Billy admitted that his hair was "a little longer" than it had been the year before—a full inch over the collar. He was identifying with the younger generation, those most likely to respond to the gospel. Amid the conflict between parents and their young people over appearance, Billy said, "It's ridiculous for parents to engage in bitter battles with their children over the haircut issue ... long hair or short hair is a matter of personal taste, not a basic moral question." He recalled that his grandfather, a Civil War veteran, "had a beard down to his chest and a mustache and very long hair ... and he was one of the most wonderful Christian men I ever knew."

Pesky Distractions

Not surprisingly, Billy faced many possible distractions—large and small—during his career. Early in his career, his charisma and good looks led to an offer from Paramount Pictures to become an actor. He declined. In the late 1950s, NBC offered him a million dollars a year to host a show opposite the highly popular Arthur Godfrey. He turned it down.

Grady Wilson describes a time in the 1960s when Graham was swimming with President Lyndon Johnson at Camp David. The president said in front of several staffers, "Billy, I think you ought to run for president when I'm finished with my term. If you do,

I'll put my entire organization behind you." Billy answered with a laugh, "Mr. President, I don't think I could do your job."

"Billy, I know you think I'm joking," said the president, "but I'm serious. You're the one man who might turn this country around."

Later, Billy revealed that President Richard Nixon offered him an ambassadorship, a cabinet post, "any job I wanted." Earlier in 1952, Texas billionaire H.L. Hunt offered Billy $6 million if he would run for president. As attractive as these options may have been, Billy realized they were not part of his mission. To each he said, "God called me to preach, and I do not intend to do anything else as long as I live."

Clarity of Focus

During the late 1970s, after feeling stung by the revelation of Nixon's statements on the Watergate tapes (see Chapter 10), Billy had to further clarify his focus on evangelism, distancing it from even informal political involvement. "I'm out of politics," he said in an interview in 1981, partly as a reaction to the perception that he had been too involved in politics through his friendships with Lyndon Johnson and Richard Nixon. He clearly separated himself from the Moral Majority, a movement that sought to steer America's political path to the right, saying:

> I'm for morality, but morality goes beyond sex to human freedom and social justice. We as clergy know so very little to speak out with such authority on the Panama Canal or the superiority of armaments. Evangelists cannot be closely identified with any particular party or person. We have to stand in the middle in order to preach to all people, right and left. I haven't been faithful to my own advice in the past. I will be in the future.

Billy openly admitted he had allowed some blurring of his focus in the past. "It was a mistake," he said, "to identify the kingdom of God with the American way of life."

After that, he would frequently respond to questions about politics with, "I'm not for the left wing or the right wing. I'm for the whole bird."

John Akers, one of Billy's closest aides, said, "Billy's principle was that you shouldn't do anything that would shut the door to the gospel. I can't tell you how important that is. People constantly want him to sign a petition about something, and he declines. He's been called a moral coward for not taking this stand, or that stand, or the other stand. But from his standpoint, to do so was to unnecessarily close doors to the gospel."

Strange Mission Partners

Having clarified his primary mission, Billy could welcome help from others, even from some who differed on other issues. This became the source for some of the most vocal criticism directed at Billy Graham over the years. Only his laser-sharp understanding of his central calling enabled him to navigate these issues.

One example arose during his 1987 meetings in Denver. Colorado Governor Richard Lamm was a platform guest on opening night. Lamm was known as a liberal Democrat who had made controversial statements about euthanasia and the obligation of the terminally ill to expedite their deaths, thus freeing up resources for others.

Graham's longtime media/public relations director A. Larry Ross remembers that this generated a lot of controversy. Many people were asking, "Why is Mr. Graham endorsing the governor? Why are you allowing him on the crusade platform?" Over and over Larry had to explain, "We're not endorsing the governor; rather, the governor is endorsing Mr. Graham and these meetings. He's welcoming us to the community and saying, 'This event is a good thing for this city and our state; we welcome Billy Graham to Colorado.'"

Billy's clarity of focus allowed him to stay on mission as he also built bridges with some unlikely allies.

The Obstetrician's Role

During his 1954 campaign in London, Billy Graham made a huge impact. Specifically he impressed British commentator George Scott, who said, "If the people will not go to the Church, the Church must go to the people.... One of the strongest things in [Graham's] favor, the fact most likely to overcome the national prejudice against him, is that he does not pretend to be a one-man Church. He sees his mission primarily as that of the fairground barker who will first win the eyes and ears of the public so that they will be attracted into the tent." Billy knew what he was called to do, and he also knew the limitations of that calling.

Billy's associate Rick Marshall used another arresting image to describe the limits of Billy's role. Marshall said that Billy was much more like an obstetrician than a pediatrician. "I have four children," Marshall explained. "They each had an obstetrician, but I only got two things from the OB—a baby and a bill. I never expected the OB to treat my children as they grew up." Billy, the spiritual obstetrician, understood where his role started and ended. But at the same time, he appreciated the many pastors who, like pediatricians, would be required for the subsequent follow-up care.

According to this image, Billy's calling was focused: He helped open people's eyes to see the work of the Holy Spirit and trust Christ as Savior, leading to a spiritual new birth. But the Christian life doesn't end there. The road of discipleship is a lifelong journey, and so Billy partnered with pastors and local churches to disciple new believers. In other words, Billy was clear about his role, and he trusted others to fulfill their roles. In fact, the Graham organization developed a vital partnership with a Christian ministry called the Navigators, a parachurch group that focused on discipling new Christians in their faith.

Preaching the Gospel in All Things

"What impresses me most about Billy Graham," said Richard John Neuhaus, former president of the Religion and Public Life Institute, "is his discipline. He sticks to what he believes God is calling him to do. His life reflects the apostle Paul's 'Woe to me if I do not preach the gospel of Christ.'"

Larry Ross said, "One of the distinctives of Mr. Graham's ministry has been his ability to make positive points for the gospel in any situation. You can ask Billy Graham how he gets his suits dry-cleaned on the road, and he'll turn it into a gospel witness."

This discipline led to Billy preaching the gospel of Christ in all things, great and small. When he received the Congressional Medal of Honor at the White House in 1996, Billy's speech was not focused on himself. Of course, he took several moments to talk about what an honor the award was and to say thank you to the important people in his life. But he spent the majority of his speech doing what he always did: preaching the gospel.

Graham noted that America has many good qualities, but he asked if the first recipients of this award would recognize the society they sacrificed to establish. "I fear not," he said. "We have confused liberty with license—and we are paying the awful price. We are a society perched on the brink of self-destruction."

Speaking on Psalm 23, Graham pointed to three causes of our national woes: emptiness, guilt, and the fear of death, which haunts our souls. "I believe the fundamental crisis of our time is a crisis of the spirit," he said. "We have lost sight of the moral and spiritual principles on which this nation was established—principles drawn largely from the Judeo-Christian tradition found in the Bible."

Graham said the country's hope is found in spiritual rebirth, and he gave a three-fold challenge: "First we must repent; second, we must commit our lives to God and to the moral and spiritual truths that have made this nation great; and third, we must translate that commitment into action—in our homes, neighborhoods, and society," he said.

As always, Billy couldn't let an opportunity pass to fulfill his mission.

CHAPTER 5
BIRTHING DREAMS

Leadership experts James Kouzes and Barry Posner argue that there is one primary attribute that distinguishes leaders from non-leaders: Leaders are forward-looking. Or more specifically, leaders can envision what Kouzes and Posner call "exciting possibilities" and then enlist others in a shared view of the future.

In an article in the *Harvard Business Review*, here's how Kouzes and Posner summarized an extensive research project about the main difference between leaders and colleagues:

> The number one requirement of a leader—honesty—was also the top-ranking attribute of a good colleague. But the second-highest requirement of a leader, that he or she be forward-looking, applied only to the leader role. Just 27 percent of respondents selected it as something they want in a colleague, whereas 72 percent wanted it in a leader.... No other quality showed such a dramatic difference between leader and colleague.[xiii]

Based on the conclusions of Kouzes and Posner, Billy Graham was clearly a leader with vision. He didn't just generate "exciting possibilities"; he also enlisted others in sharing those possibilities for the sake of the mission.

Of course Billy Graham had limitations of time, energy, and resources, yet somehow he was continually calling his team, his colleagues, and other Christian leaders around the world to adopt fresh visions for how they could spread the gospel in word and deed. In the early 1950s, for instance, Graham traveled to war-devastated Korea with Bob Pierce, endorsing his do-something-now vision for a suffering world. Today the organization Pierce founded, World Vision, is the planet's largest relief agency. Billy became personally engaged with countless ministries, including established institutions such as the Salvation Army or new ministries like Greater Europe Mission or TransWorld Radio. His multifaceted approach had many results. More than twenty-five evangelical organizations in Europe alone started as the direct or indirect result of Billy's meetings and influence.

Billy also directly spun off or became a primary catalyst for new enterprises. In 1979, even before the televangelists' scandals broke into the nation's consciousness, Billy and his organization took the lead in forming the Evangelical Council for Financial Account-ability, which now effectively monitors hundreds of member organizations.

In 1974, Billy launched a daunting new vision: He convened the International Congress on World Evangelization held in Lausanne, Switzerland. The Congress, which included 2,700 representatives from over 150 nations, was designed to draw attention to the need for world evangelization and grapple with principles, methods, tools, and strategies. The event produced the Lausanne Covenant, which combined an emphasis on evangelism and social action as the means to heal the societal wounds of racism, hunger, and poverty. That document became a guideline for ministries around the world. Lausanne, and a follow-up event in Manila in 1989 (Lausanne II), helped mobilize Christians to the cause of "Calling the Whole Church to take the Whole Gospel to the Whole World."

In addition, Billy's passionate vision to encourage evangelists in developing countries led to three large international gatherings in Amsterdam in 1983, 1986, and 2000. More than 10,000 from 185 countries and territories participated. The Amsterdam Affirmations brought encouragement and clarification to leaders from many cultures and resulted in the Biblical Standard for Evangelists, which established guidelines still used today.

An enduring and significant example of Billy's entrepreneurial vision and tenacity was the founding of *Christianity Today*. He grasped the strategic necessity of birthing the publication and concluded that he personally needed to become the driving force to bring this dream into reality. By recruiting and mobilizing, by inspiring and prodding and doing his homework, he built the momentum necessary for a successful launch and long-term survival.

But all of Graham's greatest accomplishments started with his ability to create a compelling vision and then to invite others into that vision.

The Power of Listening

During Billy's travels in the early and mid-1950s, he listened to hundreds of pastors and other Christian leaders. "Billy doesn't just meet with people to impress them or convince them," said one colleague. "He listens. Billy listens—because he's always learning."

Over and over he sensed a significant vacuum. As he later said to supporters, he found many evangelical leaders "confused, bewildered, divided, and almost defeated in the face of the greatest opportunity." A diluted, "demythologized" theology seemed to captivate many major denominations and institutions. As Billy listened to the discouragement among his evangelical colleagues, he felt compelled to take action.

For example, it was Billy's heartfelt listening that forged his passionate vision to train evangelists from around the world. In his autobiography Billy shares the unforgettable story of meeting a humble evangelist from Botswana. In response to Billy's gentle prodding, the man shared about his ministry of traveling, often on foot, throughout Botswana to share Christ. Billy asked, "What is your background? Did you go to Bible school or get any education to help you?" The man said, "Well, actually, I got my master's degree from Cambridge University."

Billy was stunned by this man's willingness to return to Botswana, completely content to follow Christ as an evangelist. Through listening to ordinary people like this African leader, Billy opened his heart to the needs around him. This deepened and strengthened the intensity of his vision.

Problems or Opportunities

Leaders can easily get so enmeshed in problems that they completely miss what Kouzes and Posner called "exciting possibilities." But in his role as a forward-thinking vision-caster, Billy was able to identify problems and challenges and, rather than get bogged down in discouragement, turn them into opportunities for ministry. In the words of leadership guru Peter Drucker, Billy was able to convert these "opportunities" into "results."[xiv]

Certainly this was how Billy approached the "problem or opportunity" that led to the start of *Christianity Today*, which initially launched in Washington, D.C., before moving to the Chicago area. During the launch process, there were additional opportunities to turn into results. For instance, when Billy was seeking wisdom and support among his ministry and business allies, they assumed the new publication would be published by his own organization. Certainly that was the simplest way to fulfill this vision. To create a separate board and separate location and facilities would take lots of additional effort, both short- and long-range. But Billy was convinced that the offices should be located in Washington, a strategic city for the launch of a national publication of influence. He wanted a separate board of directors and staff, with leadership from the academic, ministry, and business communities to give it credibility.

Two visionary moments that topped Billy's list of achievements—his 1983 and 1986 International Conferences for Itinerant Evangelists—also started with a problem. Billy describes how his overseas work left him humbled by the high quality of leadership in other cultures. He was struck by the heroic service he observed, but he saw a need: These dedicated Christian men and women desperately needed training, encouragement, and resources. After much research and prayer, Billy and his team sponsored two conferences that trained and inspired what Billy called a "multinational, multiracial, multilingual, multidenominational throng" that "sang, prayed, studied, and witnessed as one in Christ."

Stormy Weather

Of course, vision requires change, and change is almost always difficult. John Maxwell bluntly states this truth:

> Let's face it; change is messy. [Peter Drucker] observed, "As every executive has learned, nothing new is easy. It always gets into trouble." ... Unfortunately, most people don't see change as a gift. But it is. Every time you embrace change, there is an opportunity for you to go in a positive direction.... Without change, there is no innovation, creativity, or improvement.[xv]

Certainly that was true with the launch and first years of *Christianity Today*. Billy's dream required money, and a lot of it. He wasn't overly optimistic that adequate funds could be raised. When he tried to enlist business leaders, he found them interested but noncommittal. He told J. Howard Pew, head of Sun Oil, that he "was giving more thought to the possibilities of this magazine than to any other single thing in my life." He sensed that if Mr. Pew got on board, the dream might become reality. Pew eventually agreed to provide significant funding for the first two years. Still, *CT* struggled financially in its first years, but Billy weathered the storm by persistently soliciting funds from businessmen.

He also elicited the help of seasoned veterans. Drucker says the only effective means to bail out new endeavors when they run into "heavy weather" is to have "people who have proven their capacity to perform."[xvi] That's why a new dream can't rely on rookies, no matter how smart or highly motivated. It takes veterans who have been through tough times themselves and won't be shaken when thunderheads roll in. Billy knew *CT* was an important project, so he built a critical mass of strong leaders with deep commitments to see the projects through. Billy recruited leaders like his father-in-law, L. Nelson Bell, who had started an influential Presbyterian magazine, and Harold Ockenga, president of Fuller Seminary and pastor of historic Park Street Church in Boston, along with key businessmen to serve as trustees. With their help, Billy navigated the choppy waters during *CT*'s early years.

Right People, Right Seats

The chapter in Jim Collins' *Good to Great* titled "First, Who ... Then, What" emphasizes the vital importance of getting "the right people on the bus (and the wrong people off the bus)." He also advises, "Put your best people on your biggest opportunities, not your biggest problems."[xvii]

But in developing a new concept and "putting legs under it," how does one connect, identify, and recruit? When Billy launched *Christianity Today*, he was in a unique position to recruit the right people. His meetings throughout the country put him shoulder-to-shoulder with both lay and pastoral leaders. He and his staff worked with the community's leading Christian business people and ministers in each city. This gave him up-close impressions of how they thought, what they could accomplish, and how committed they were to mutual dreams. Over the years after *CT*'s launch, Billy would personally recruit new trustees to achieve the desired mix of business and ministry leadership.

To birth a dream takes lots of recruiting skill, and Billy was always a recruiter, connecting with strong people and thinking about how they might best move the cause forward. It's true that at times he recruited too hastily, carried along with enthusiasm as he saw a person's strengths that hid some weaknesses. But as his associates say, he had a solid overall track record for getting the right people in the right places.

In the late 1970s, for example, *CT* was in a major transition, and a search had begun for a new magazine editor. Billy had observed Kenneth Kantzer's capacities as a theologian and leader and decided he was the man. Ken had largely built Trinity Evangelical Divinity School over a period of years and brought to the table a loving spirit, leadership experience, a quick mind, and a Harvard PhD.

When Billy approached Ken, however, the educator politely declined. Kantzer felt he was most effective in academia, and he didn't believe he was equipped to become *CT*'s editor. Yet Billy kept returning to his original premise—that Ken was the man. He contacted Ken again and was again politely refused. But Billy persisted, and finally, months later, Ken said yes. Dr. Kenneth Kantzer made enormous contributions to the magazine during his years as editor, and after he returned to Trinity, he continued to work with *CT*'s leaders on many projects. Billy had gone with his gut and brought the right person onto the bus.

Continual Improvement

When the first issue of *CT* came off the press in October 1956, Billy read it thoroughly. He also spent time reviewing it with others he respected. Then he wrote Carl Henry, the magazine's first editor-in-chief, a lengthy—and blunt—synopsis and evaluation. Reporting on his research with others, Billy wrote, "Almost all have agreed that the content was not strikingly good, considering the terrific roster of editors and correspondents. They all seem to feel that the magazine may be slanted a little too much to the 'egghead,' and there aren't many eggheads among ministers. Particularly did I receive almost unanimous criticism of the editorial pages. I, too, would agree that there was not enough ring of joy, strength, and good news."

Concerning the book reviews, he reported, "This is where we received probably our greatest criticism. One said, 'Minor League stuff.'" One critic said the attempts at humor were "terrible." Another said the humor looked like "a man with no sense of humor trying to be humorous."

But Graham also reported praise for several articles. And he was brutally honest about his own article, reporting that one reviewer said, "It was a bit too much spinning dust and purple prose." Having criticized his own work, he then said that Carl Henry's article was a wonderful idea, but that others called it "too verbose." One man used the expression "obscurity reaching for profundity."

Billy concluded by writing, "Now, my beloved Carl, do not let any of this discourage you.... Personally I was delighted with the magazine." Then Billy went on with pages of practical suggestions and also cautions about being as inclusive as possible without compromise. Henry soon wrote back with appreciation for his insights.

When the second issue was published, Henry received yet another letter, this one brief and congratulatory. Billy was no mere cheerleader; he was a strategist, a "positioner," a theologian—not in a scholarly sense but in the essentials. Years later one *CT* editor commented, "I don't know how I would have felt if, after editing that first issue, I'd received that letter from Billy Graham. It certainly would have captured my attention—and would have let me know exactly what he was thinking."

Make No Little Plans

Ever since *CT* was launched, it has launched numerous other magazines—some successful, some not. Along the way, some magazines were discontinued because they were not financially viable. But as Billy demonstrated so often, dreaming big—even with its pain and failure—is better than shrinking into a safety mode that is pain-free but leads nowhere.

David Burnham, an early twentieth century American architect and city planner who developed the master plans for a number of cities (including Chicago and downtown Washington, D.C.), once said:

Make no little plans. They have no magic to stir men's blood and probably themselves will not be realized. Make big plans. Aim high in hope and work, remembering that a noble, logical diagram once recorded will never die, but long after we are gone will be a living thing, asserting itself with ever-growing insistency. Remember that our [children] and [grandchildren] are going to do things that would stagger us.[xviii]

Billy kept choosing to make "no little plans." Instead, he aimed high with noble visions. As a result, his life and his accomplishments still "stir men's blood."

CHAPTER 6
FUNDING THE MISSION

An online survey conducted by a New York law firm found some disturbing trends among the 250 financial professionals they interviewed. A little over half of the professionals surveyed felt it likely that their competitors had engaged in unethical or illegal activity to gain a market edge. Nearly a third of the respondents believed that financial services professionals might need to engage in unethical or illegal activity in order to be successful. And 24 percent said that they would probably engage in illegal insider trading to make $10 million if they could get away with it. The survey concluded:

> A particularly troubling and consistent finding throughout the survey is that Wall Street's future leaders—the young professionals who will one day assume control of the trillions of dollars that the industry manages—have lost their moral compass, accept corporate wrongdoing as a necessary evil and fear reporting this misconduct.[xix]

Money is something that organizations, companies, and ministries desperately need to accomplish important goals. When used well, it can be a powerful tool for growth. But it is easily the downfall of many leaders, creating a dangerous lust for more. Throughout his ministry, Billy Graham saw both money's potential and temptation, but he managed to leave a solid track record of financial success and integrity.

In an article for *Outcomes* magazine Harold Myra wrote:

> We respect Billy Graham for many things, including his financial integrity. Yet we can easily think that was more or less automatic for him—that he just handed off the responsibilities to businesspeople with a charge to be honest. But financial integrity is never simply a given. It is hard fought and hard won, and in today's wrenching economy, dangers and temptations loom larger than ever.[xx]

Billy's team structured their ministry to reinforce guidelines and hold themselves accountable, giving the board authority and accepting its supervision. This approach was based on Billy's perspective about money, aptly summed up by this statement: "If a person gets his attitude toward money straight, it will help straighten out almost any other area of his life."

Billy's brother Melvin said, "I've never seen a man in my life that cares as little about money as Billy does." This is evidenced by the fact that Billy has given away millions of dollars of royalties and said no to countless offers to enrich himself. But Billy and his team worked hard to fund their mission. And once they raised those funds, they released their financial resources for the sake of spreading the gospel and equipping other leaders to share the gospel. In other words, they aligned their financial resources in accord with their mission.

Setting the Financial Tone

Billy Graham's integrity is well recognized by many leaders and celebrities, both Christian and non-Christian. When they wrote their Modesto Manifesto, Billy and his trusted leaders identified money as a huge stumbling block for leaders. In fact, it was the first point in the manifesto they crafted. From that time forward, Billy set a tone of financial transparency and accountability that has trickled down throughout his ministry and into the lives of those he leads.

If asked about Billy Graham and money, most people might assume his high-capacity business advisers handled all that for him. In some respects that was true, but as CEO, and as the man who had to answer questions from the press, and from his own conscience, he knew he carried the ultimate responsibility.

Graeme Keith said that Billy was the first to admit business was not his strong suit. Yet everyone on the board took their cues from Billy because he displayed a high level of trust and financial transparency. "We all felt his charge," Keith said, "and it made you want to work for him. After Billy gives you a responsibility, you feel that sense of trust he has in you. Integrity is critical. He sets the expectations."

One of the ways Billy set the tone in his ministry was by connecting with donors. Billy said that he thought his greatest contribution to the organization was writing regular letters to his supporters. At first glance, that statement might seem a bit jarring. Billy Graham's greatest contribution was writing fund-raising letters? Yet Billy's observation fits. He understood that resourcing the organization was vital. The letters were pure Billy Graham in tone and substance.

His sensitivity to the danger of coming off like a salesman meant that he faithfully wrote those fund-raising letters not just for the money but to communicate with authenticity. Billy did what he did best: He built his constituency and made sure trustees and managers were in place to cover all the financial bases. The kind of tone he set for his organization was contagious to everyone who worked with him, and it was ultimately his financial integrity that helped fund the mission to spread the gospel to the ends of the earth.

High Standards
Just as it is important for leaders to personally set the tone for financial growth and integrity, it is also valuable for leaders to set high standards for the organization as a whole. Billy Graham and his team repeatedly insisted on high standards for their organization, and this started with a sobering incident after the 1950 crusade in Atlanta. The day after the event ended, an Atlanta newspaper ran two photos: one of Mr. Graham smiling as he departed, and the other of his aides struggling to carry away the bulging money sacks containing that day's "love offering." Nearly thirty years later, Billy reflected, "Was I an Elmer Gantry who had successfully fleeced another flock? Many might just decide that I was."[xxi]

Because of its global impact, the Billy Graham Evangelistic Association has been under scrutiny for many years. A 2002 article in *The Dallas Morning News* reported, "From the IRS to professional auditors to independent observers of large philanthropies to the individual donors that contribute most of the annual budget, plenty of people keep an eye on the organization."

Yet, even when so many other organizations and ministries were exposed in financial scandals, the Graham organization was founded on transparency from the beginning. "They continue to this day to be a leader in accountability," said Dan Busby, vice president for member and donor services for the Evangelical Council for Financial Accountability. "Their track record across the decades speaks for itself."[xxii]

According to officials from the Billy Graham Evangelistic Association, at one time the average donation received was under twenty-eight dollars. These humble sacrifices, when added together, equaled millions of donations that made up the majority of the organization's budget. That indicates the level of trust and the emotional bond between Mr. Graham and millions of donors, said Rebekah Basinger, a fund-raising consultant for Christian organizations. "I've never run into a donor who says they feel misled or manipulated or strong-armed by the Graham organization," she said. "Even though it's a very large organization, and a lot of the people who are giving have never even met someone personally from the organization, they feel a real sense of emotional and spiritual attachment."[xxiii]

Billy and his team worked for many years to maintain and show their financial integrity. In 1979, after a series of public scandals concerning other well-known ministries, the BGEA was among the co-founders of the Evangelical Council for Financial Accountability. An executive from the BGEA and one from World Vision worked together to set up the council. Designed to be a "Better Business Bureau" for Christian organizations, the council now has more than 1,000 members, a true testament to Mr. Graham's leadership in this area. Billy's organization has taken an active pursuit of transparency that allows for scrutiny and investigation.

Appearances Matter

Not only did Billy and his team display financial transparency, they also made a commitment to avoid any appearance of financial impropriety. They knew that the way a leader lives—or even appears to live—speaks volumes about financial integrity. Over the years, Billy Graham laid a proven track record of personal and organizational integrity and frugality. That track record was crucial in communicating the gospel to people from different socioeconomic backgrounds.

He was even careful about what kind of cars he was seen driving or traveling in. His brother Melvin said, "Unless he was with somebody like President Kennedy, he wouldn't even want to use a limousine." Billy had an intuitive grasp of how people might react to symbols of wealth (like a limo), which was probably informed by his upbringing. Because Billy experienced the Depression as a young man, a frugal attitude became permanently imprinted into his behavior.

Sterling Huston, who served as director of North American ministries for the BGEA, recalled an example of Billy's concern for financial appearances. Many years ago some of his board members offered to buy him a plane and pay for all expenses so he wouldn't have to fly on commercial flights with all the hassle. "Billy," they said, "you don't have to worry about all this. This won't have to come out of the budget; we'll take care of it." However, Billy later called the chairman of the executive committee and said, "I can't do it. I haven't slept all night. I know it's paid for, but people just won't understand."

"It wasn't that it was improper," Sterling explained. "The apostle Paul said, 'All things are lawful,' but not all things speed the gospel along. Billy's sense of that truth was more important to him than his own comfort."

Part of what Billy was reacting against may have been what he outlined in the Modesto Manifesto. He and his colleagues had seen many leaders fall. Tragic examples of leaders who used money selfishly made him viscerally opposed to feathering his own nest. Although he had many wealthy friends, he was acutely aware of the Bible's warnings about the love of money, and he was determined not to become personally entrapped. His own skills with money were unexceptional, but he saw money as a vital, God-given asset to be wisely employed. And, he knew that, even with the best of intentions, financial sloppiness could spell disaster.

Kingdom Generosity

"Kingdom generosity" refers to a spirit of caring about the work of God's kingdom beyond your organization's focus. It's a spirit that moves leaders beyond institutional survival or success into a willingness to support other ministries that are also doing vital kingdom work. Billy Graham was focused on this kind of generosity for many years.

One of the biggest ways in which Billy demonstrated kingdom generosity was through the World Emergency Fund, a ministry dedicated to global crises and needs. This ministry was founded in 1973 after Billy's travels brought him face-to-face with the shocking reality of human suffering on a global scale. Billy witnessed millions of people living in abject poverty, hunger, or illness. For instance, in 1977 a cyclone and tidal wave hit the Indian state of Andhra Pradesh, destroying hundreds of villages and leaving 100,000 people dead. Billy was already in the area for a crusade, so he was able to visit one of the devastated villages. A man ran up to him, grabbed his legs, and hung on as he shouted, "Kills us or help us rebuild!" Through the World Emergency Fund the Graham organization took that cry literally. They rebuilt an entire village, creating 285 cinder-block homes and a 500-seat church building.

One of the earliest tragedies the World Emergency Fund aided was the Guatemalan earthquake in 1976. After the earthquake devastated the country, Billy visited to witness the wreckage, see how he could help, and encourage pastors and leaders in Guatemala City. They partnered with local Christian agencies to bring relief in the form of food, medicine, and other necessities.

The World Emergency Fund has ministered to countries affected by crises all over the world. Billy sums up his call this way: "We know we cannot do everything that needs to be done, but in a world that is never free of turmoil, Christ calls us to do what we can."[xxiv]

Wise Counsel

Billy Graham didn't just rely on his own financial integrity; from the beginning, he surrounded himself with a strong team of advisers. Although Billy was the driving force in generating the revenues, he consistently accepted the board's role in making financial decisions. Many CEOs with Graham's access to power, privilege, and fame would have used those opportunities to meet their own needs, but not Billy. With his team of high-capacity, mission-minded trustees, he welcomed genuine partnership and proper board dynamics. This allowed them to handle even the most difficult issues and to ensure both accountability and effectiveness.

George Bennett, who served as both the treasurer for Harvard and for the Graham organization, said, "I've never known an organization that has better financial management than the BGEA. How that happened, I don't really know, except that Billy had an outstanding ability to pick the right people. They had outstanding financial control."

Picking the right people is easier said than done, but once Billy did that, he was able to develop a deep level of trust with his leadership team. This trust cultivated a healthy and safe environment to discuss a sensitive issue like money.

A Realistic View of Money

In a 1999 article for the *St. Louis Post-Dispatch*, Billy noted the limitations and dangers of money: "Money can buy a bed, but not sleep; finery, but not beauty; a house, but not a home; books, but not an education; medicine, but not health; religion, but not salvation."[xxv]

And yet Billy Graham and his organization also used money for God's purposes. Billy was able to tie money to a compelling vision to share the gospel. One example comes from Ted Engstrom, who later served as president of Youth for Christ and then World Vision. He was chair of Billy Graham's very first citywide meetings in Grand Rapids, Michigan, in 1947. "In 1948 he came to our city to raise funds for me to go and participate in the Youth for Christ World Congress on Evangelism," Ted said. "Billy was willing to personally make sure the vision was resourced."

Throughout his ministry Billy understood both the value and danger of money. He led from a sense of integrity, but he was also willing to take risks for the sake of the vision.

PART THREE
TEAMWORK

"Teamwork is always at the heart of great achievement," says *New York Times* best-selling author John C. Maxwell. "The question isn't whether teams add value. The question is whether we will acknowledge that fact and work to become better team players."[xxvi]

Billy acknowledged the value of teamwork very early in his ministry. In fact, the phrase "the team" became a shorthand way to highlight the fact that this wasn't just Billy Graham's ministry. The ministry belonged to "the team."

This section explores two aspects of teamwork that undergirded Billy's ministry success. Chapter 7 focuses on the "inner circle" of the Graham organization, including his rich and long-standing partnerships with people like George Beverly Shea, Cliff Barrows, and brothers Grady and T.W. Wilson. Chapter 8 looks at Billy's commitment to mentor aspiring Christian leaders and evangelists from around the globe. Over the years, Billy taught, inspired, and trained literally thousands of men and women in the way of following and serving Christ.

This section also emphasizes that Billy wasn't just a team-builder; he was also a humble, committed team member. For Billy, teamwork was always a two-way street. In other words, he learned from his teammates, he leaned on his teammates, and his faith was inspired by his teammates.

CHAPTER 7
FORMING THE TEAM

Since 1995, when the movie *Toy Story* was released, Pixar has created eleven feature films, all of which have become huge international successes. From its beginnings as a production company, Pixar has focused on the crucial value of teamwork and collaboration. Steve Jobs, Pixar's co-founder and chief executive, moved everything— including mailboxes, meeting rooms, a coffee bar, and even bathrooms—into the center of the atrium so people would be forced to interact. Initially, some of the employees complained, but Jobs kept telling Pixar employees, "Everybody has to run into each other." A Pixar producer called it "smooshing" and added, "If I don't see lots of smooshing, I get worried." It was Jobs' way of empowering others.

Brad Bird, the director of *The Incredibles* and *Ratatouille*, eventually caught the vision for teamwork. Bird said, "The atrium initially might seem like a waste of space ... but Steve [Jobs] realized that when people run into each other, when they make eye contact, things happen. So he made it impossible for you not to run into the rest of the company." It's no surprise, then, that the Latin motto for Pixar says it all: *Alienus Non Diutius*, or "Alone No Longer."[xxvii]

Although Billy never used that exact phrase, it's clear that his entire approach to ministry followed the same motto—"alone no longer." For the most part, he became a household name primarily because of his incredible gift of evangelism. However, another one of Billy's gifts was finding, encouraging, and empowering teammates to fill the right positions for fruitful ministry.

In contrast to today's team-focused leadership models, when Billy was starting his ministry, rigid hierarchical models were the norm. This was the period when business guru Peter Drucker conducted his study of General Motors, which showed how often rank-and-file followers feel devalued and disempowered by management. Over the next four decades, Drucker wrote brilliantly about leading others by forging a sense of teamwork. But when Billy first started forming his team, the wealth of today's insights about participative leadership were largely undiscovered. Billy didn't simply form an outstanding team; he led it in such a way that its core members stayed by his side for nearly a lifetime.

In most organizations the odds are often stacked against long-term teams. The team leading an organization must confront failures and adapt to successes; handle its own personnel disputes within the team; adjust strategies to brutal new realities; adapt to growth, resistance, and reversals—an endless list of dynamics that disrupt trust and bruise egos. Highly effective teams are tough to form and tougher to keep intact over the long haul.

Against the odds, however, Billy's original team stayed together as the BGEA ministry burgeoned, related organizations were founded, and the pace accelerated. For nearly sixty years of exciting but grueling ministry, the health of their teamwork proved to be the foundation for their longevity and success.

The Doctrine of Chemistry

Bill Hybels once said that, after many years of experience, he became "a convert to the doctrine of chemistry." Hybels has concluded that the personality of each team member represents one of the top factors in building a great team. It was this powerful, positive chemistry between Billy and his close associates that made decades of effectiveness possible.

Billy had the advantage of testing the chemistry of potential teammates for years before his team was formed. When he worked for Youth for Christ in the 1940s, he traveled incessantly, speaking and engaging with pastors, YFC directors, and other leaders of the emerging evangelical movement. During this time, he not only deepened his convictions and refined his strategies, he also began sensing who would become his ministry "soul mates."

By the fall of 1947, Graham was ministering in a campaign in Charlotte, North Carolina, with his core team: Cliff Barrows, Grady Wilson, and George Beverly Shea. But because Barrows matched Graham in spiritual intensity and platform charisma, it wasn't easy for them to find the right chemistry. Graham biographer William Martin explained the challenge:

> For Cliff Barrows, becoming the second member of the Graham/Barrows campaign team meant the subordination of his own ministry to Graham's. Such a subordination was not easy. … Cliff was a gifted preacher, and he and Billy combined talent, enthusiasm, transparent sincerity, and a remarkable lack of egotism into a highly winsome package. They clearly had the option to remain in a leading role with YFC or to establish their own independent evangelistic ministry, or to get off the road and serve as pastors.

Even years later Cliff Barrows confessed, "I struggled with that decision for a couple of years, because I wanted to pursue preaching." The financial uncertainty of relying on the "love offerings" given to traveling evangelists was also a deterrent. But eventually, after praying and weighing all the factors, Barrows says, "The Lord told me, 'Do the music for Billy and whatever has to be done, and I'll take care of the preaching opportunities."

Cliff told Billy, "Bill, you know the struggle my wife and I have had about whether we join your team, and the Lord has given us peace in our hearts. As long as you want me to, I'll be content to be your song leader, carry your bag, go anywhere, and do anything you want me to do."

Barrows recalls that Graham said, "May we serve together until the Lord returns, or until one of us is called home to heaven." That decision marked the beginning of a remarkable team, composed of two men who recognized that their strengths were complementary rather than competitive. Together they could accomplish more than either could alone.

From the time of his conversion in Charlotte, Billy had also been close to the Wilson brothers, Grady and T.W., and at various times held meetings with them. In Chicago he met George Beverly Shea and recruited him to be his musical soloist. These men, along with Cliff Barrows, became his core team. He knew he not only could work with them but they could bond together. It was the chemistry between Billy and his close associates that energized decades of ministry effectiveness.

Cliff Barrows said that Billy always put the team's success ahead of his personal success. "He is a friend of the team," Barrows said. "He spoke of the team and team activities as 'ours,' not as 'me' or 'mine.'"

Good chemistry usually strengthens over time, but there is one caveat: Time spent working together doesn't necessarily guarantee good teamwork. A good team works increasingly well together because they learn to blend their principles and personality. They learn to anticipate one another's reactions and handle the inevitable surprises in a coordinated way. For example, business leader Fred

Smith once watched the Graham team at work during a campaign when a guest musician performed too long. "I watched Cliff and Billy," he said. "They didn't even need to exchange words. Just a glance between them was enough to signal a slight change of plan in response to what was happening."

As a leader Graham demonstrated that bringing on soul partners lifts any enterprise or ministry. In contrast, the wrong chemistry can blow up the best-laid plans.

Flaws and Weaknesses

Grady Wilson, who Billy called "my God-given balance wheel," said, "[Billy] is painfully aware of his humanity—he has flaws, and he's the first to admit them." Billy didn't try to hide what he couldn't do. His candor about his inadequacies made his team well aware of both his strengths and his weaknesses.

By contrast, many leaders often hide their weaknesses as they try to instill fear instead of love in their followers. But a leader without admitted weaknesses provides no opportunities for teammates to make a significant contribution.

Billy found a balance between leading and following. For instance, at a Christianity Today International board meeting, he commented in response to a suggestion, "I don't think my board would allow me to do that." Though he led his board, and though the trustees looked to him for leadership, he also deferred to them, believing that "in the multitude of counselors there is wisdom." His wife, Ruth, also became a key adviser to Billy on numerous crucial issues. On multiple levels, he sought accountability as protection and a source of wisdom that created clear parameters for decision making.

In his autobiography, Billy openly expressed how much he needed this band of "heaven-sent" teammates:

[They] propped me up when I was sagging and often protected me from buffetings…. They did not back away from correcting me when I needed it or counseling me with their wisdom when I faced decisions. I'm convinced that without them, burnout would have left me nothing but a charred cinder within five years of the 1949 Los Angeles Crusade.[xxviii]

A Merry Heart

When one hears laughter in the halls of an organization, when good spirits enliven the breaks, when serious discussions are broken up by humor, it's a very good sign the enterprise is healthy. Teams that emphasize fun and good spirits lift effectiveness.

One biographer included an entire chapter on humor in the Graham team. The chapter, appropriately titled "Laughing All the Way to Heaven," described practical jokes played on each other and Billy's good-natured acceptance of jokes played on him. Of course, at times Billy could initiate the good-natured practical jokes as well. Although extremely serious about their mission and the eternal stakes, the team knew how to laugh together and play together. Billy could especially laugh at himself, even when under the spotlight or on camera when he had blown a line.

For instance, he liked to tell of the time in a small town when he asked a boy how to get to the post office. After getting directions, Billy invited him to come to the meeting that evening. "You can hear me telling everyone how to get to heaven." The boy's response? "I don't think I'll be there. You don't even know your way to the post office."

The Book of Proverbs sums it up: "A merry heart does good, like medicine." And Billy said, "A keen sense of humor helps us overlook the unbecoming, understand the unconventional, tolerate the unpleasant, overcome the unexpected, and outlast the unbearable."

The Power of Focused Attention

Large challenges energize and unite teams. In sports, preparing for the Super Bowl or the World Cup has an amazing effect on concentration, energy, and determination. Urgency, direction, mutual accountability, and respect all blend as every team member determines to seek the highest performance possible.

But all of this starts with the leader. Business leader Jim Collins writes, "There is a symbiotic relationship between great institutions and great [leaders].... The [leader] is transformed by committing to a bigger purpose than mere personal success, and in doing so, the [team] is transformed into greatness."[xxix] This certainly personified Billy, whose burning purpose was authentic and evident to every one of his teammates.

It helped that Billy's team knew beyond the shadow of a doubt that he was not in it for his own glory. They sensed his humility, and they also understood the price he paid for playing his role on the team day after day, year after year. At times Grady would have to step in for Billy at the last minute to preach or hold a press conference. Knowing how the press could spin anything, and how the slightest misstep could wound Billy's ministry, Grady felt the pressure. Once, after standing in for him, he told Billy, "I never realized what you go through night after night, standing before large crowds in these great auditoriums and stadiums. I'm a nervous and physical wreck after each time I've had to substitute for you."

When the goals are clear, each team member understands how to contribute, and each team member has burdens to bear and challenges to confront. They're willing to do whatever it takes because they share the same vision, the same goal.

Pastor and author John Ortberg contends that the success of Billy's team flowed primarily from shared goals, or what Ortberg called "the power of focused attention." Ortberg writes:

> Churches and other organizations regularly spend months if not years these days standing around white boards trying to craft a purpose statement, then go through the same process all over again every time top leadership changes. So it is almost humorous that the Billy Graham Evangelistic Association's purpose statement was written ... [in] a single sitting because it was demanded by the paperwork needed to start a nonprofit organization in 1950: To spread and propagate the Gospel of the Lord Jesus Christ by and in all ... means. What made it possible to write so quickly, of course, is that the organization and its namesake had a commitment to a single direction that makes a compass needle look fickle.

Critics could argue about the team's approach or philosophy, but no one could deny the Graham team's unswerving tenacity to spread and propagate the good news of Jesus Christ.

The Jazz-Band Leader

Larry Ross uses a musical metaphor to describe Billy's style for choosing and empowering others to utilize their gifts in the great mission of sharing the gospel. According to Ross, Billy was much more like a jazz-band leader than a symphony conductor. Symphony conductors merely mount the podium and lift a baton, and all the musicians raise their instruments to play. But the jazz-band leader "stands in front of the ensemble tapping his foot to set the rhythm. He'll points to the piano player to take a few bars; then he points to the saxophonist, and he does a riff. They're all playing the song, but at different times different people take the lead doing different things, which enhances but doesn't eclipse the group's overall sound."

The Graham team became strong because Billy acted like the leader of a jazz band, showing the way but giving each member ample opportunity to exercise significant responsibility. In other words, Billy placed confidence in God and the members of his team. As Cliff Barrows said:

He sought God's will; he was God-dependent, motivated by his love for God and man. He was self-effacing, but he was secure in the place of God's appointment. He was anointed of God, [but] he was considerate. He was not authoritarian. He knew that in the multitude of counselors there is safety. His decisions were based on mutual agreement rather than on a dictatorial basis. He thought about and relied on the counsel of those he trusted. He was never demeaning or reprimanding. He trusted people and respected their contribution.

Cliff also said Billy's refusal to micromanage stimulated positive team chemistry.

One of my greatest resources these sixty years is the clear sense of Bill's backing and support and his belief in me and other members of the team. He respected the gifts God gave us. He never interfered with those who worked under him. He trusted the Lord and the choices he made of leaders. As a result, we would have—and did—follow him anywhere God led. We would even have laid down our lives for him.

David Schmidt, media consultant for the BGEA, called this aspect of Graham's commitment to teamwork "cascading trust." In other words, Billy trusted those around him, and those people in turn found people they could trust. Schmidt said:

> When you have a great leader, and his character and worldview cascade through the enterprise, the enterprise can accomplish great things! Billy surrounded himself with people who cared for him, told him the truth, and got results. He modeled the bonding. For Billy to trust others, he had to be trustworthy himself. That meant loving others and telling the truth. Billy delivered on his promises and got results. All that challenges me to do the same.

William Martin said that what impressed him most when he talked with people who had worked with Billy over the decades was the way he selected and delegated. "He chooses people whom he trusts," Martin said, "then delegates a great deal of the authority to do the task. Their own dedication to him and confidence in him causes them often to rise to the occasion."

No Rock Stars

One of the marks of a great leader is the ability to give credit where credit is due—even when it means humbling oneself to raise up others in the organization. Throughout his ministry, Billy Graham often took time to share the credit in big and small ways. As William Martin said:

> Billy not only delegates authority, but he gives credit to those who do their jobs and shares the credit very generously; that makes others feel appreciated. They have confidence he is what he claims to be—that he is a man of integrity and he's not going to disappoint or embarrass them. All this lifts them to a higher

level. Carl Henry told me, with a kind of chuckle, "When Billy asks you to do something, you kind of want to find a way to do it. You don't want to let him down."

Not only did Billy raise leaders to new heights of leadership and excellence, he also behaved with great humility, even when others treated him like a celebrity. David Schmidt said:

> I wish I could help [people] understand what it's like to have the state and local police pull up in a motorcade and escort you to the lower bowels of a stadium through a back door. There's so much that says, "You, you, you. You're a rock star! You're it!" Billy goes down the line shaking hands, meeting dignitaries, and everything is saying, "You're important." But Billy kept saying, "No, it's not for my glory. God won't share his glory, so I need to get down so he can get up." When you have a leader at the top who says, "This is not about me," that's big!

The unique gift that Billy had to raise others to a higher standard resonated throughout his organization. It flowed from his deep humility and his insistence on giving others the praise that they earned.

"The Team"

John Ortberg notes, "There are a handful of people who have sustained [Billy Graham's] level of fame for that stretch of time; of those it is difficult to think of any that have retained the same leadership team over decades of challenge and transition. This kind of stability does not happen by accident."

Indeed, the phrase "the team" permeated the Graham organization. Though it refers to the inner circle of leaders, "the team's" spirit of unity and cooperation radiated out to everyone throughout the organization. The team spirit extended to thousands of participants. It even extended to volunteers and local leaders who made the crusades happen in their hometowns. A counselor or coordinator, a team member or recruiter felt like a vital contributor, fully engaged, following the playbook, working in tandem with the players who were up front and leading the process.

CHAPTER 8
MENTORING OTHER
LEADERS

On October 14, 2012, the Austrian skydiver Felix Baumgartner broke two world records that had stood for over fifty years. He smashed the previous world record for the fastest dive, reaching a velocity of nearly 834 miles per hour. He also broke the world record for the highest freefall, jumping from 128,000 feet, or twenty-four miles.

But the forty-three-year-old Baumgartner gladly admits that he couldn't have done it without the help of his mentor—the previous world record holder for both records, eighty-four-year-old Joe Kittinger. Months prior to Baumgartner's record-breaking dive, Kittinger provided him with advice and encouragement whenever the younger man doubted his ability. Kittinger's reassuring voice from mission control guided Baumgartner throughout the dive, especially during one particularly tense moment when Baumgartner started spinning out of control—the same problem that had nearly killed Kittinger during his dive.

When the dive was finished, Kittinger had only praise for Baumgartner's new world records. Kittinger said, "Felix did a great job, and it was a great honor to work with this brave guy." Baumgartner also had nothing but praise for his mentor, saying, "It feels like if Joe's there, nothing can go wrong."[xxx]

One of the most profound effects of Billy's leadership involved the way he mentored other Christian leaders, igniting a fire in their hearts for gospel-centered ministry to the world. He wasn't building his own empire; he was building something bigger. The fires he ignited have had lasting impacts all over the world in the lives of leaders, churches, and parachurch organizations.

Sometimes, Billy ignited fires in very small ways. For example, Jay Kesler, former president of YFC, was deeply impacted by Billy's leadership, even though they only interacted a few times. A few years after Kesler became YFC president, Billy was holding a crusade in Rio de Janeiro and YFC was also meeting there. Billy and Jay were in the same hotel, so when Billy went up to the roof to get some sun, he asked Jay to join him. "While he was resting and recuperating, we talked for a couple of hours about the challenges of youth ministry," Jay remembers. "He's a good listener, and I felt affirmed. He encouraged us to stay focused on evangelism and avoid the secondary issues: eschatology, various denominational differences, modes of baptism, and all the political things."

Kesler's example speaks volumes to Billy's mentoring relationships, the way he invited others to learn from his years of wisdom and ministry lessons. From the micro to the macro scale and everything in between, Graham had had a passion for building up other leaders in a variety of contexts, equipping them for the work God had called them to and strengthening his own ministry in the process.

A Vision for Mentoring

Because Billy Graham had such a wide global influence throughout his ministry, he wasn't always able to mentor upcoming leaders on a one-on-one basis. And yet, at times, in the ordinary course of ministry, Billy unintentionally had a profound impact on other leaders. For instance, David Schmidt said:

> The DNA [of the Graham organization] was mission-focused, and full of compassion. They always treated me lovingly … if firmly. No one's perfect; we make mistakes and have to be corrected. You must work hard. You won't be kept if you're deadwood. But the focus was on the cause. You can't do that if you don't see cause and compassion blended in the leader. We didn't need to meet personally with Billy on projects because we could emulate that blend of cause and compassion. Our entire firm's motivation stayed intense.

In other words, for Schmidt and other leaders, Graham's ministry genius was caught rather than taught. But Billy also knew he had to become more intentional about teaching other leaders the important lessons of his ministry experience. He needed a clear vision for mentoring.

That heightened intentionality came in the early 1960s when Dr. Victor Nelson, a retired pastor and trusted adviser to the Graham organization, visited Billy when he was speaking in Nova Scotia, Canada. Dr. Nelson challenged Billy to hone a clear vision for mentoring younger leaders. "Billy, if you just puddle-jump from crusade to crusade all over the world," Nelson said bluntly, "you'll never accomplish what you could and should accomplish. You not only need to do this work yourself, but you need to multiply your efforts. You need to train others to do effective evangelistic work also."

At the time, Billy said he knew Dr. Nelson was right. Billy wrote in his autobiography, "In spite of an almost nonstop crusade schedule, I sensed that we needed to work toward an international conference on evangelism." Actually, this conversation sparked something that was already starting to burn within Billy's soul—a vision to mentor and train other itinerant evangelists from around the globe.

A Plan for Mentoring

A vision always must be brought into reality. After Dr. Nelson's bold challenge, Billy had to make a plan for his passion for mentoring other leaders. First, Billy saw the need. He noticed that there was no real worldwide network—formal or informal—to train, equip, and encourage evangelists. Second, in the mid-1960s he started laying the groundwork for a number of international conferences. These plans would eventually lead to the Berlin Conference (1966), Lausanne '74, and the two International Conferences for Itinerant Evangelists (1983 and 1986), both of which were held in Amsterdam.

The first Amsterdam conference, which brought together leaders from all over the globe, provided an incredible opportunity to make his mentoring vision a reality. Here's part of the stirring challenge he offered the evangelists who had assembled:

We are the first generation that has the awesome capacity to destroy mankind from the face of this planet because of the development in incredible weapons of mass destruction. But we also have within our hands the technological breakthroughs in communications that make it possible to reach every corner of the earth with the gospel in this decade. Let us therefore ask God to give us fresh vision. It may be painful for us to face the failures of our lives honestly and confess them to God, but may God break through the barriers in our hearts and minds to strengthen our hands, to enlarge our vision, to be used of God for his glory and his joy.

This vision spilled over to the attendees. One attendee in particular, evangelist and apologist Ravi Zacharias, remembers this conference with great fondness: "The role of these more than 10,000 evangelists was ennobled and honored. They returned to their nations encouraged and equipped to make a difference."

Even though Billy wasn't able to offer each of these leaders one-on-one mentoring, he gave them the gift of incredible vision. According to Zacharias, this had a powerful impact on his ministry, and undoubtedly, over thirty years later, it continues to echo in the lives of leaders and organizations around the world.

The Power of Encouragement

Jay Kesler has noted that Billy's inner circle of leaders exuded a spirit of encouragement that overflowed and impacted other aspiring Christian leaders. Kesler said:

> The whole Graham organization and all their people were tremendously encouraging to me. The best metaphor is King Arthur. The Knights of the Round Table had deep affection for and loyalty to Arthur. Billy is the combination of about ten people who gave over their whole lives and careers to reach the world for Christ. I've never been around a Billy Graham insider who spoke with anger or envy or disillusionment about their involvement in the Association. They're not fawners or sycophants or courtiers, they simply have a shared vision.

Sherwood ("Woody") Wirt also experienced Billy's ability to encourage younger leaders. A few months after Billy invited Wirt to join the staff, Graham's meetings started drawing huge crowds in Australia, and he brought his new editor into the thick of it. Once, although he wasn't invited, Woody joined the team's travel roster for a flight to Tasmania. He felt apprehensive that he'd been too bold, and on boarding the plane he met Billy, who was surprised at his presence.

However, Billy reached over and laid his hand on Wirt and encouraged him with an encouraging welcome. "Bless your heart," Billy said.

Billy didn't use his leadership position to exclude Wirt; on the contrary, he encouraged Wirt with open arms, ensuring that he held a place of leadership and trust in Billy's circle of influence.

At one point in his career, Wirt interviewed a prominent person, and then sent the edited version to the interviewee—who strongly objected to a deletion. Woody agreed that the deleted material wasn't acceptable, but he faced an immediate deadline, so he went ahead and published the interview without including the deletion.

When that issue of *Decision* came out, the man was furious. He immediately called Billy to object. In responding to the irate man, Billy didn't put Woody in a bad light. He told the man that he'd always seen his editor act with integrity, and then Billy apologized for the incident. In a later discussion with Woody, he reassured him, but he also counseled, "Next time, Woody, don't get caught so close to the deadline. Protect yourself."

As this story shows, encouragement doesn't preclude personal challenges. Soon after hiring Wirt to edit *Decision*, Billy sent him a letter stressing the high stakes of the magazine. "These early issues," he wrote, "will be of strategic importance, as they will be analyzed and studied by religious leaders around the world. I hope you will put the best of everything into it." He challenged Wirt, as he challenged other leaders he mentored, to aim high and not accept something that was less than their best.

Breaking Racial Lines

At some point mentoring new and promising leaders in God's kingdom necessitates crossing lines of race and culture. One of Billy's greatest cultural battles focused on the issue of race.

Jay Kesler remembers that decades ago YFC was trying to chart a course on the race issue.

> [Graham's] example was so important to us. Up until then, in the conservative Christian world, we believed that to deny the gospel was a sin, but to deny the social justice issues was just kind of a mistake. Watching Billy, we saw that we needed to put them both in the same category—that one without the other was truncated. One could be as deeply disobedient to Christ over social issues as one could be over theological issues. That's what made us new evangelicals.
>
> He integrated his campaigns and brought into his organization associate evangelists who were black. We saw what Billy did, and we too in the 1960s platformed black leaders such as Bill Pannell and Tom Skinner. On the cover of our teen magazine, *Campus Life,* we ran a photo of white and black teenagers riding in the same convertible. We had hundreds of magazines sent back from groups that would not distribute it in the South. But we were committed to this, and Billy's example confirmed for us that this was the right direction.

In the early 1950s, a few years before Martin Luther Jr. and the civil rights movement garnered the national spotlight, Graham talked about the church's obligation to overcome the race problem in America. "The ground at the foot of the cross is level," he said, "and it touches my heart when I see whites standing shoulder-to-shoulder with blacks at the cross."

To be sure, Graham was never at risk of being mistaken for a civil rights activist. At times he moved cautiously (too cautiously and not cautiously enough for some of his critics), taking incremental steps on controversial matters. Still, for a white evangelical of his stature to put the issue of race relations on his ministry's agenda was quite remarkable.

The Results of Mentoring

The connection between Billy Graham and Ravi Zacharias was mentioned earlier in this chapter as an example of the impact that Billy Graham has had on other leaders. Ultimately, many of these connections have happened not through one-on-one relationships, but through the resources the BGEA has been able to offer leaders around the world.

Ravi Zacharias remembers the 1983 conference in Amsterdam as such an occasion of being resourced for his ministry:

> There was no one else in the world who could have brought about a conference like that, raising the resources for it, and elevating the work of the evangelists of the world. He didn't need it, but we did. If you ask anyone who attended, even if they don't remember any of the messages, they remember the people they met and the networks they established. It opened up so much of the world to me. My whole ministry took a dramatic turn after that. Invitations to speak poured in from many parts of the world. But in addition, two other things happened at the conference.
>
> First, I was made aware that a vast majority of evangelism was being done to reach "the unhappy pagan," the person whose life is falling apart and who is ready to grasp the gospel because it offers hope for their painful situation. I realized there are large numbers of people who are not unhappy, who find their lives fulfilling, at least apparently so, and I sensed the need for someone, maybe me, to speak to "the happy pagan." From Amsterdam, my wife and I went to India, where we saw the

great need of pastors there, and I told my wife, "I would love to be an evangelist to the skeptic, to the honest intellectual who has intellectual objections to faith. I'd like to develop that kind of Christian apologetic ministry."

Second, I remember Billy Graham saying, "You have never evangelized a person until you have told them about the cross." Billy told of a difficult moment when he preached and had no response whatsoever. Then one of his colleagues put his arm around him and said, "Billy, you ought not be surprised. There was no cross in your sermon tonight."

Later, when I told Leighton Ford about these reflections, Leighton said, "Billy has always maintained that it's fine to reach the intellect, but if you lose the simplicity of the gospel, you will not accomplish the task." I knew that was the way to go. I'd seen God take Billy, an honest man with integrity and a simple trust in the profound power of the gospel, and I said, "That's what I want to be." The Lord used Billy Graham and the Amsterdam conferences to light a fire way beyond what he ever imagined.

Ravi Zacharias went on to launch a ministry to skeptical intellectuals, with offices in Atlanta, Toronto, Oxford, Singapore, India, and Abu Dhabi. Young leaders need to be mentored and taught, but they also need the resources that connected leaders can offer. Billy was able to offer these resources, which ultimately made a big impact on the mission of the gospel in the twentieth and twenty-first centuries.

Mentor and Mentored

Billy's mentoring didn't just go in one direction. In his humility and commitment to keep growing as a leader and a disciple of Christ,

Billy often learned from his protégés. John Huffman, chairman for the board of Gordon-Conwell Seminary, recalls, "What surprised me was how through the years he would invite me to play a round of golf, or call me up at almost any time of the night or day with some question or insight he had, even asking for help on a message he was preparing—treating me not as a person twenty years younger, but graciously and humbly asking for my counsel. He never came across as someone who had all the answers and was dispensing them to the next generation, but in the process, he was both a voice of wisdom and a mentor."

Billy was also profoundly moved and challenged by the faith and commitment of the itinerant evangelists who attended his conferences. After the first Amsterdam ICIE, Billy wrote movingly about the delegates who arrived barefoot and without a change of clothes. In a profound way, Billy describes learning from "an itinerant evangelist to Stone Age animists in Irian Jaya [who] sold all the pigs that were his means of livelihood in order to raise money to attend the conference."

It's not a surprise, then, to hear Billy's praise for the very ones he wanted to mentor. "These itinerant evangelists ... are a mighty army of proclaimers, energized by the Holy Spirit, spreading across the world with a renewed vision to reach their own people for Christ."

PART FOUR
CHALLENGES

John Ortberg asserts that every living creature needs challenges to spur new growth. Ortberg writes, "We require change, adaptation, and challenge the way we require food and air. Comfort alone will kill us." Ortberg offers a specific example: "When teachers want students to grow, they don't give them answers—they give them problems!"[xxxi] Based on this truth, Ortberg asks, "Is it possible that we actually need adversity and setbacks—maybe even crisis and trauma—to reach the fullest level of development and growth?"[xxxii]

Leaders grow the same way—by accepting the reality of challenges. This section examines three common leadership challenges that confronted Billy Graham throughout his life and ministry—criticism, betrayal, and failure. Like us, Billy didn't relish these challenges, nor did he seek them out. All three challenges came to him, over and over again. But when they came, he didn't flee from them. He faced them head-on, and the challenges spurred new growth not just for him, but for his entire ministry as well. In the process, Billy offers us a profound leadership lesson: Somehow adversity leads to growth in a way that nothing else does. Rightly accepted, challenges cause leaders to grow into the best version of themselves.

CHAPTER 9
APPRECIATING CRITICS

November 19, 2013, marked the 150th anniversary of President Abraham Lincoln's "Gettysburg Address." According to a 2013 editorial in *The New York Times*, this brief speech (272 words, two minutes long) still has the power to "do what words are rarely able to do: invoke an eloquent silence." The same article adds, "There is an overpowering immediacy in these plain words."[xxxiii]

At the time of the speech, the majority of newspapers praised it, but Lincoln's words didn't escape scathing criticism. *The Harrisburg Patriot* derided Lincoln's address by referring to his "silly remarks." *The New York World* accused Lincoln of "gross ignorance or willful misstatement" with his declaration of "four score and seven years ago." The Democratic-leaning *Chicago Times* observed, "The cheek of every American must tingle with shame as he reads the silly, flat and dishwatery utterances of the man who has to be pointed out to intelligent foreigners as the President of the United States." *The Times* of London commented: "The ceremony [at Gettysburg] was rendered ludicrous by some of the sallies of that poor President Lincoln."[xxxiv]

It just goes to show that you really can't please all of the people all of the time. In other words, people who have vastly different leadership styles and who lead vastly different organizations will have at least one thing in common: They'll get criticized.

Deserved or undeserved, criticism hurts. Today our culture conditions us to amplify our reactions to criticism. Polarizing political debates, heated talk news shows, abrasive sitcoms— numerous sources urge leaders to respond to criticism with anger and revenge.

Billy Graham's strategy was the polar opposite of this dark undercurrent. The British Christian leader John Stott once said, "[Billy Graham] has loved his enemies who have vilified him, bearing the pain and declining to retaliate." To even his harshest critics Graham genuinely reached out in love. As a result, he redeemed many volatile situations and empowered his own soul.

Of course at times Billy Graham still got angry with his critics. But throughout his ministry years, he displayed a remarkable pattern in dealing with even his harshest critics.

The Reality of Criticism

Billy Graham's life demonstrated that if a leader is moving in the right direction, he or she will attract critics. Leadership, by definition, means change, which makes criticism inevitable. Billy accepted the reality of criticism rather than let it become a threat.

Throughout the years Billy was stung by deeply personal and unfair barbs, taunts, and stings. On different occasions he was described as being a "moral dwarf" and "psychologically sick." They said he told "sanctified lies." His prayer at a presidential inauguration was termed a "raucous harangue." A liberal seminary compared his ministry to a "spiritual rape." Religious fundamentalists were just as critical, condemning his "compromised" ministry that tried to reach out to Roman Catholics and mainline Protestant groups.

His moderate anti-segregationist stance during the Civil Rights era drew fire from both sides. White segregationists were furious when he invited the "agitator" Martin Luther King Jr. to pray at the 1957 New York City crusade. Civil rights activists accused him of cowardice for not joining them on protest marches and getting arrested for the cause.

A conservative ally broke from Billy and then told a local television station that Billy was "doing more to harm the cause of Christ than any living man." Meanwhile, from the other end of the theological spectrum, the prominent theologian Reinhold Niebuhr condescendingly asserted that Billy Graham's "solution" to contemporary problems was "too simple in any age, but perhaps particularly so in a nuclear age with its great moral perplexities."

As John Ortberg observed, "One challenge the Graham team has had to face at almost unprecedented levels is how to respond to criticism." But rather than viewing criticism with shock or dismay, Billy accepted and expected it. Jerry Beavan, an early Graham associate, recalls the time he was upset at someone who had attacked Billy. "I was really mad," he told us. "I was talking to Billy and said, 'Bill, they can't say these things about you!' He said, 'Jerry, they're not talking about you! Why should you get mad?' Billy stayed positive."

Unapologetically Mission-Focused

Early in his ministry, Billy Graham and his team made a crucial decision about how to spend their emotional energy: They decided to focus on the mission, not critics. In 1952 Billy said, "Satan would like nothing better than to have us stop our ministry and start answering critics, tracking down wretched lies and malicious stories. By God's grace I shall continue to preach the gospel of Jesus Christ and not stoop to mudslinging, name-calling, and petty little fights over nonessentials."

The team did their best to stick to that commitment. On one of Graham's European preaching tours, for instance, the great Swiss theologian Karl Barth took Billy mountain climbing and then attended one of the crusades. Barth said he agreed with most of the message, but he didn't like the whole idea of the "invitation" and he told Billy to drop the word *must* from the line "You *must* be born again." But when Emil Brunner, another influential Swiss theologian, heard the same message, he disagreed vehemently. "Pay no attention to [Barth]," he said. "Always put that word *must* in there. A man *must* be born again." Bruner urged Billy to keep giving the invitation as well.

As President Lincoln learned after the Gettysburg Address, leaders can't please everyone. So Billy and his team consistently and intentionally tried to avoid focusing on fickle human opinions. Instead, they focused on their God-given mission.

As Pastor Leith Anderson has noted, in the long run, Graham's ministry greatly benefited from this pursuit of mission. Anderson wrote:

> Unlike many religious leaders before and since, Graham refused to attack his critics.... Most of those people and their issues have long been forgotten, but Graham's legacy is long-lasting. If he had chosen to attack those with whom he disagreed he would have been lost in the dust of forgotten controversies.

As critics howled, Billy kept clear about the mission. As a matter of fact, Billy would frequently hear out a critic, patiently explain the mission, and then unapologetically ask his critic to join him.

Surprise Your Critics

On numerous occasions Billy Graham disarmed his critics by offering them kindness rather than vengeance. During his 1947 preaching campaign in Birmingham, England, Billy faced intense opposition from skeptical local pastors. Through the years, these local pastors had watched itinerant preachers breeze into Birmingham, leading revivals while they denounced the local clergy. So before he even arrived, they were convinced that Graham was just another religious opportunist.

But Billy took a different approach. He made personal appointments with his detractors, admitted his weaknesses as a young preacher, and assured them that he only wanted to help them reach their city for Christ. Soon the local hostility morphed into support. One of the local pastors who was initially critical of the meetings said:

> Billy called on me...[and] I ended up wanting to hug the twenty-seven-year-old boy.... I called my church officers, and we disrupted our plans for the entire nine days. Before it was over, Birmingham had seen a touch of God's blessings. This fine, lithe, burning torch of a man made me love him and his Lord.

A few years later in Los Angeles, a local pastor criticized Graham's upcoming meetings because they were already disrupting his church services. For eight weeks straight the pastor called the team to complain that his work was being hindered and that Billy didn't care about local churches. Billy patiently tried to explain that he was trying to help, not hinder, the local churches.

Finally, on the last weekend before the meetings started, Billy called the pastor and said, "Sir, I want to thank you for the leadership your church has provided in this series of meetings, and you would do me a great honor to sit with me on the platform. I'd like to introduce you and ask you to lead in prayer." The pastor was overwhelmed. He told Billy that if he ever preached within 100 miles of his church, he would be there, as would his congregation.

Billy continually applied a simple but powerful principle: The best way to get rid of a critic is to turn the critic into a friend. For Billy, this principle usually worked.

The School of Criticism

Some leaders embrace controversy, seeing it as a means to prominence and press coverage. Billy did not. Instead, he tried to meet with his critics so he could learn from them. Critics can force leaders to evaluate what they really believe about themselves and their mission. As Lon Allison observed about Billy, "His preferred mode is to go directly to the people causing him the most pain and basically say, 'Teach me.'"

For instance, when Reinhold Niebuhr published one of his many disdainful critiques on Graham's theology and approach to ministry, Graham responded with a humble desire to grow and improve. At one point, he replied, "When Dr. Niebuhr makes his criticisms about me, I study them, for I have respect for them. I think he has helped me to apply Christianity to the social problems we face."

When Niebuhr rebuffed Graham's attempts for a private meeting, Billy simply complimented him. He told a group of reporters, "I have read nearly everything Mr. Niebuhr has written, and I feel inadequate before his brilliant mind and learning.

Occasionally I get a glimmer of what he is talking about." But Billy also had a subtle message for Niebuhr: "If I tried to preach as he writes," Graham said, "people would be so bewildered they would walk out."

Although Niebuhr never met with Graham, time and again Billy would take the initiative to arrange personal meetings with his critics. Nearly every time, Graham's humility, transparency, and genuineness would melt their resistance.

Two Simple Sentences

Billy, unlike some leaders, wasn't afraid to use two simple sentences: "I was wrong" and "I am sorry." Billy never groveled, but he wasn't afraid to humbly admit his faults, even in the heat of unfair criticism.

During his 1954 London meetings, Graham's organization faced blistering attacks before they stepped on British shores. To raise money for the trip, the team had produced a fund-raising brochure in the United States that gravely offended the host country. Billy's aides had unknowingly used language that criticized Britain's ruling Labour Party. The London *Daily Herald* pounced on the mistake by running the following headline: "Apologize, Billy—Or Stay Away!" A British journalist chimed in, "Billy Graham has more gravely libeled us than anyone has dared to do since the war."

Although alarmed and discouraged by the damaging publicity, Billy employed the same tactics that had so worked so well in Birmingham. He surprised his critics with a prompt and clear apology for the fund-raising brochure snafu.

Journalists learned that they had misjudged him. A local writer confessed:

To be honest, I was prejudiced about him. We have heard so much here about these American hot gospellers and their methods of selling religion, which they seemed to have picked up from the salesman of insurance. And then, just after breakfast yesterday, I met him. I had better say straight away ... I may be making a mistake, but I think he is a good man. I am not so sure he isn't a saintly man. I just don't know. But make no mistake about this ... Billy Graham is a remarkable man.

Amid the frenzy of the same 1954 crusade, Billy also sent a brief note to William Conner, who had harshly criticized him in the *Daily Mirror* newspaper. He diplomatically complimented Conner: "While your articles about me were not entirely sympathetic, they were two of the most cleverly written that I have ever read."

He offered to meet Conner, who accepted and impishly suggested they meet at a pub called "Baptist's Head." Following the meeting Conner said, "I never thought that friendliness had such a sharp, cutting edge. I never thought that simplicity could cudgel a sinner so damned hard. We live and we learn.... The bloke means everything he says."

What won over these hard-edged journalists? Apparently it was Billy's willingness to take the initiative and first admit *his* faults. As a result, although the team feared the bad press would drive people away, instead for twelve weeks audiences packed every venue where Billy preached.

The Long-Term View

Chapter 3 told the story about Graham's controversial and much-maligned preaching trip to the Soviet Union in 1982. Despite meeting with persecuted Christians, Graham was quoted as saying that he "had not personally seen any evidence of religious persecution." Although some labeled him a "traitor," Billy insisted that he would go anywhere to preach as long as he could freely proclaim the gospel. When he returned to the United States, he claimed he saw the hand of God in the Soviet Union. He was fiercely attacked for being a naive "tool of the Soviet propaganda machine."

It would take nearly a decade to vindicate Graham to his critics. In 1990, after the fall of the Soviet Union, then-President George H.W. Bush praised Billy for his ability to detect the first stirrings of religious freedom behind the Iron Curtain of communism. Bush argued that:

> It takes a man of God [like Billy Graham] to sense the early movement of the hand of God.

At times, based on a short-term viewpoint, all the critics might seem right. But Graham's life shows that God isn't just interested in the "short term." That's why the psalmist urges us to "be still before the Lord and wait patiently for him" (Psalm 37:7). Sometimes a leader's mission only becomes clear after a long season of waiting on God with perseverance.

Christlike Response

During the 1954 London crusade, Graham had the unique opportunity to meet C.S. Lewis in the dining room of St. Mary Magdalene's. Graham reports that as they parted, Lewis warmly told him, "You know, you have many critics, but I have never met one of your critics who knows you personally."[xxxv]

That's a good summation of Billy's relationship with critics. While he was never completely free from criticism, he demonstrated that critics don't have to destroy us. They don't even have to demoralize us. Our first reaction to our critics may be to blast them. But an effective leader looks for the opportunities this opens up and develops alternative strategies. A courageous, intelligent, and Christlike response to criticism can lift us and our critics to a new level.

CHAPTER 10
FACING DISAPPOINTMENT
AND BETRAYAL

Mary Karr, poet and author of *The New York Times* best-selling memoirs *Lit* and *The Liars' Club*, described herself as a "black belt sinner and lifelong agnostic." But in 2009 she surprised the literary world by embracing Christian faith. In a recent interview, Karr offered the following insightful reflection about living with flawed people in a fallen world:

> I don't think any of us get off this planet without suffering enormously. And one of the chief ways we suffer is by loving people who are incredibly limited by the fact that they're human beings, and they're going to disappoint us and break our hearts…. Your parents—no matter how great their marriage was, at some point it trembled in its foundation, and it was terrifying. [Or] you fell in love with someone who didn't love you back. Or whatever. We are all heartbroken. It's the human condition.[xxxvi]

"We are all heartbroken." And the heartbreak usually comes from someone who loved us and disappointed us. Karr has identified the sting of relational disappointment or betrayal.

Many leaders would say their most painful experiences focus on a story of betrayal. Someone they fully trusted, someone with whom they had let down their guard and become fully vulnerable, betrayed them. In a survey of pastoral leaders, *Leadership Journal* found that about 60 percent had experienced at least one leadership-based traumatic betrayal. The vast majority said they had been hurt by persons they thought they could trust.

Although Billy's dedicated inner circle modeled unity, civility, and teamwork, he didn't escape from betrayal's heartbreak. At some point, to use Karr's words, betrayal caused his life to "tremble in its foundations." And when it did, Billy faced a hard truth of leadership: How you respond to the wounds of betrayal makes the difference between becoming a vital leader or a wounded, bitter leader.

Billy started to learn this lesson early in his life. In the winter of 1938, Emily Cavanaugh said yes to Billy's marriage proposal. But a few months later, Emily broke off the engagement and returned his ring. Billy was devastated. He told a friend, "All the stars have fallen out of my sky." To make matters worse, not long after the breakup, Emily started dating a young man named Charles Massey, an older student who at the time seemed destined for more success than Billy would ever achieve.

Yet, the abrupt change in marriage plans taught Billy an important lesson about God's good purposes even in the midst of human disappointments. William Martin writes: "Night after insomnia wracked night [after the engagement broke up], he stalked the streets of Temple Terrace or roamed the lush, humid countryside for three and four hours at a time, praying aloud as he walked."[xxxvii] Finally, after wrestling with God in prayer, Billy reached a decision. On the eighteenth hole of a golf course, he knelt and prayed, "All right, Lord, if you want me, you've got me…. I'll go where you want me to go."

Through the loss of a valuable relationship, Billy had found his call to preach the gospel. And once he put his hand to the plow, he never looked back.

Shock and Dismay

According to his wife, the most painful thing Billy experienced during his ministry was the realization that President Richard Nixon, a close friend and ally for decades, had deeply betrayed his trust. They became friends when Nixon was vice president under Dwight Eisenhower. When Nixon lost the presidential election to Kennedy in 1960, and two years later lost the election for governor of California, he was devastated. Once excruciatingly close to the Oval Office, Nixon sank into depression. It seemed that only a few still believed in Nixon. His devoted friend, Billy Graham, remained true to Nixon.

"Dick, I believe you'll have another chance at the presidency," Billy told Nixon as they played golf together. Billy's respect for Nixon was genuine and deep. He admired his intellectual capabilities and government expertise. In 1967, Nixon called Billy for advice. The political tide had turned once again. Down and out for five years, Nixon had reclaimed much of his earlier luster. Now he wanted Billy's opinion on making another run for the White House, so he invited Billy to join him in Florida.

During two days in Key Biscayne, Nixon and Billy discussed Scripture and prayed, as they frequently did when together. Shortly before Billy left, they walked along the beach, discussing Nixon's aspirations. Nixon pressed Billy for guidance. "You still haven't told me what to do," he said. "If you don't run, you will always wonder if you should have," Billy replied. "I will pray for you, that the Lord will give you the wisdom to make the right choice." Later, Nixon said that Billy, more than any other individual, influenced his decision to run.

On election night, before appearing victoriously to the press, Nixon invited Billy to join his family in the hotel. When Billy arrived, Nixon asked everyone in the room to join hands so Billy could pray. Such outward manifestations of spirituality impressed Billy. Their many conversations convinced him of Nixon's genuine, if still private, religious belief. Halfway through Nixon's first term, Billy wrote his old friend a note: "My expectations were high when you took office nearly two years ago, but you have exceeded [them] in every way! You have given moral and spiritual leadership to the nation at a time when we desperately needed it—in addition to courageous political leadership! Thank you!"

On January 21, 1969, Nixon was inaugurated as the thirty-seventh president of the United States. Nearly four years later he was reelected in one of the largest landslides in American political history. But shortly after his reelection, the Nixon presidency started to unravel, largely due to a complex web of scandals summed up by the word "Watergate." The word specifically refers to the Watergate Hotel in Washington, D.C., where five men broke into the Democratic National Committee headquarters. The scandal eventually landed forty-three people in prison, including dozens of Nixon's top administration officials. As the scandal unfolded, it was revealed that President Nixon had recorded numerous conversations about his cover-up attempts. Eventually the Supreme Court ruled that Nixon had to turn the tapes over to the authorities. On August 8, 1974, under the imminent threat of impeachment, Richard Nixon became the first U.S. president to resign. By the time he left office in disgrace, Nixon had turned the White House into a thuggish criminal enterprise.

It all came to light when the American public finally heard and read the Watergate transcripts. When Billy listened to the tapes he became emotionally and physically sick: He wept and vomited. Normally an astute judge of character, Billy never saw this devastation coming. He no longer recognized his friend.

Nixon's fall stung Billy so deeply because the president had betrayed him publicly as a visible ally and privately as a close friend. The association with Nixon tarnished Billy's ministry and legacy, and Billy wondered how he could have been so wrong about him. "I just couldn't understand it," Billy said, "I still can't. I thought he was a man of great integrity. I looked upon him as the possibility of leading this country to its greatest and best days. And all those people around him, they seemed to be such clean family men. Sometimes, when I look back on it all now, it has the aspects of a nightmare."

Notice Billy's initial response: He didn't just "get over it." He didn't experience instant, "victorious" feelings of joy and forgiveness. Instead, he simply felt the raw emotions of shock and dismay. Following Billy's example, healing the wounds of betrayal often starts with simple honesty about the hurt that's been inflicted on us.

The Bitterness Trap

Although he let the shock and dismay sink into his heart, Billy didn't get stuck in feelings of anger and resentment. Most leaders will have ample opportunities to stay trapped in the jaws of bitterness. Savoring bitterness is emotionally and spiritually deadly. In the midst of his heartache over Nixon's betrayal, Billy made a decision to avoid the poison of bitterness, eventually even reaching out to Nixon with love and concern.

The night before President Nixon resigned, Billy attempted to reach the president by phone, but without success. Even after Nixon left the White House in disgrace, Billy refused to shame the former president. "I shall always consider him a personal friend," he told reporters. "His personal suffering must be almost unbearable. He deserves the prayers even of those who feel betrayed and let down." Billy remained pastoral despite being chief among the "betrayed and let down." He tried to visit Nixon in California, but the former president was too sick for visitors. Undeterred, Ruth hired an airplane to fly around Nixon's San Clemente home towing a banner that read, "Nixon, God Loves You and So Do We."

The following spring, Billy finally was able to visit Nixon in California. Nixon's daughter, Julie Eisenhower, recalled:

> The purpose of the visit was simply to reassure both of my parents of his complete love and faith in them. The lack of hypocrisy and absence of a 'holier than thou' attitude had always impressed me tremendously. Dr. Graham's capacity for friendship and his eagerness to love make him stand apart from other men.

Somehow Billy took a profound spiritual journey from shock, dismay, and anger at outrageous injustice to arrive at a place of forgiveness and love. In the process, he preserved his own spiritual health.

Responsible and Faithful

How should leaders respond to the "emotional hits" that can't be denied? In the aftermath of Nixon's betrayal, Billy chose to walk in faithfulness. Though Billy suffered deep disappointment, his love for the man who betrayed his trust remained strong. When Nixon died in April 1994, Billy accepted the unenviable responsibility of conducting his funeral. The eyes of the world looked to see how

Billy would address Nixon's considerable, if severely tarnished, legacy. In his eulogy, Billy carefully acknowledged the complexity of Nixon's character. He also pointed out his stature. Then he spoke of the Nixon he had known:

> There was another more personal, more intimate and more human side to Richard Nixon that his family, neighbors, and friends that are gathered here today would know. It was a side many did not see, for Richard Nixon was a private and perhaps even a shy individual whom others sometimes found hard to get to know. There were hundreds of little things that he did for ordinary people that no one would ever know about. He always had a compassion for people who were hurting.

"When I talk about suffering," Billy said in his book *Hope for the Troubled Heart,* "I'm no different from you. I would like to live a life free of problems, free of pain, and free of severe personal discipline. However, I'd had extreme pressures in my life to the point where I've wanted to run away from reality."[xxxviii] Note the words "severe" and "extreme."

At the Cove retreat center, there is a cemetery with a designated plot for Billy. Billy said that sometimes the mental, physical, and spiritual pressures on him have been so great that "I felt like going to the Cove and lying down in the cemetery to see how I fit." Yet after that wry comment, Billy added, "God has called me to my responsibilities, and I must be faithful."

Hope from the Depths

In Psalm 130, the psalmist prays for mercy and displays hope even "out of the depths." Even in the depth of personal or corporate pain, Billy was committed to communicating hope to others.

We see that spirit in Billy as he responded to the 1995 Oklahoma City bombing. David Frost observed that although the president and the governor both spoke at the memorial service, it was Billy's words that "offered the most comfort to those who had lost loved ones." Billy clearly put himself in the place of the bereaved. "Times like this," he said, "will do one of two things: They will either make us hard and bitter and angry at God, or they will make us tender and open and help us to reach out in trust and faith.... I pray that you will not let bitterness and poison creep into your souls but you will turn in faith and trust in God even if we cannot understand."

He continued his speech with the following words spoken "out of the depths" of pain:

Some of you today are going through heartache and grief so intense that you wonder if it will ever go away. I've had the privilege of meeting some of you and talking to you. But I want to tell you that our God cares for you and for your family and for your city. The Bible says that the God of all comfort who comforts us in our troubles. Jesus said, "Blessed are they that mourn for they shall be comforted." I pray that every one of you will experience God's comfort during these days as you turn to him, for God loves you and he shares in your suffering....

There's hope for the present because I believe the stage is already been set for the restoration and renewal of the spirit of this city. You're a city that will always survive, and you'll never give up. Today, it's my prayer that all Americans will rededicate ourselves to a new spirit of brotherhood and compassion, working together to solve the problems and barriers that would tear us apart.... But there's also hope for the future because of God's promises. As a Christian, I have hope not just for this life but for the life to come.... My prayer for you today is that you will feel the loving arms of God wrapped around you and will know in your heart that he will never forsake you, as you trust him.

Billy was able to communicate hope to others because his life had "trembled to its foundations," and he chose hope and forgiveness over despair and hate.

Common Disappointments

In one of his last books, *The Journey: Living by Faith in Uncertain Times*, Billy wrote, "Life turns on us in many ways, but one experience is common to all of us: disappointment." Billy went on to say the harshest disappointments involve pain in relationships—the rebellion of a child, or a failed marriage, for instance. Often life's most heart-rending wounds stem from a deep betrayal by someone we love. But Billy urged his readers, "Unless we learn to deal with disappointment [especially the disappointment of betrayal], it will rob us of joy and poison our souls." So the most important question to ask when life turns against us is not 'Why?' but 'What?' 'What do You want me to do, Lord?... What response do You want me to make?'"[xxxix]

Of course Billy wasn't giving advice that he hadn't already learned to put into practice. We seldom think of calamities as opportunities for growth, especially when they send us reeling. But they are. In hindsight, we sometimes see that even the worst human betrayals helped us understand ourselves, shaped our character, and deepened our faith in the One who was betrayed into the hands of sinners on our behalf.

CHAPTER 11
LEARNING FROM FAILURE

R.O. Blechman, one of the most famous illustrators in the world, shared a series of letters that he wrote to a younger fellow-illustrator. In one of the most poignant letters from his book *Dear James: Letters to a Young Illustrator*, Blechman addresses the reality of failure:

> Preliminary drawings and sketches often are discouraging things, pale shadows of one's bold intentions.... "Is that what I did," the novice might ask, "and I consider myself an *artist?!*" ... My trash basket is full of false starts and failed drawings.... There should be a Museum of Failed Art. It would exhibit all the terrible art that would have ended up in trash bins and garbage cans, lost and unknown to the public life.[xl]

Illustrators, artists, athletes, and leaders have one thing in common—failure. And for leaders with a large vision, at some point, failure is inevitable. But as Blechman notes, failure isn't disastrous. To the contrary, a trash basket full of "false starts and failed drawings" is part of the process of creativity and eventual success. For the follower of Christ the goal is not a fail-safe record but a reliance on God to teach us in the midst of our most glaring failures.

Even thoughtful secular observers have recognized failure's ability to shape and develop leaders. Steven Snyder, author of *Leadership and the Art of the Struggle*, argues that "struggle and leadership are intertwined....Great leaders use failure as a wake-up call."[xli] Dean Kamen, the creator of the Segway Human Transporter and holder of 440 patents, joked that his biggest failure is "that I have too many to talk about."[xlii] In her 2008 commencement address at Harvard, J.K. Rowling, author of the Harry Potter series, extolled what she called "the fringe benefits of failure." "It is impossible to live without failing at something," she said, "unless you live so cautiously that you might as well not have lived at all—in which case, you fail by default."[xliii]

Failure's Wake-up Call

Billy was also able to acknowledge the benefits of failure—particularly the spiritual benefits. For instance, one of Billy's early failures, an embarrassing blunder following a meeting with President Truman, prepared him for a lifetime of significant encounters with world leaders. It happened in 1950, when Billy was thirty-one years old and still emerging as a national figure. After two successful campaigns in Los Angeles and Boston, Billy thought it was time to make contact with the highest levels of political power. He hoped to gain the president's support for his evangelistic efforts, especially a crusade he dreamed of bringing to West Berlin. He wrote the White House to request a visit with President Truman. Though his initial request was denied, he persisted and wrote the president's secretary. A bit later, after Communist forces invaded South Korea, Billy sent a telegram to the president. Still no luck. But, after working through Massachusetts Congressman John McCormack, Billy finally got an invitation for a twenty-minute appointment on July 14, 1950.

Billy asked that he be able to bring along three colleagues—Grady Wilson, Cliff Barrows, and Jerry Beavan. Surprisingly, permission was granted. At the end of their meeting, Billy asked,

"Mr. President, could we have prayer?" The president, not known for his spiritual side, said, "I don't suppose it could do any harm." So Billy put his arm around Truman's shoulders and prayed, while Grady and Cliff chimed in with "Do it, Lord," and hearty "Amens."

Upon emerging from the White House, the press corps descended on them: "What did you tell the president, and what did he say?" Billy, not knowing he was violating diplomatic protocol, told them everything he could remember. The next day, newspapers across the country ran stories of the meeting. "It began to dawn on me a few days later how we had abused the privilege of seeing the president," he said. "The president was offended that I had quoted him without authorization."

He tried to make amends, but Truman denied his attempts. Only many years later, while in retirement at his home in Independence, Missouri, did Truman agree to see Billy. "I recalled the incident and apologized profusely for our ignorance and naiveté," Billy said. "Don't worry about it," Truman said graciously. "I realized you hadn't been properly briefed."

Billy vowed that it would never happen again if he was given access to a person of influence. And true to his vow, after the embarrassment with Truman, he was circumspect regarding his conversations with prominent persons.

During the London meetings in 1954, for instance, Billy met privately with Winston Churchill for forty minutes. What did they talk about? Journalist George Burnham, who traveled with the Graham team, reported that the question was still unanswered a year later. All Billy would reveal during Churchill's lifetime was that it was Bible-centered.

When he was invited to preach at a private chapel service attended by Queen Elizabeth, the Duke of Edinburgh, the Queen

Mother, and Princess Margaret, he was queried by reporters about what he said. Billy revealed only that he had spoken for about twenty-five minutes and used Acts 27:2–5 as the text for his sermon.

Despite his mishap with President Truman, Billy eventually became a confidant of popes, presidents, and prime ministers because he had learned to keep conversations in confidence, and because he decided not to be paralyzed by his mistakes. In 1981, he visited for half an hour with Pope John Paul II. Afterward he would speak only in general terms of their conversation, saying that they talked about "inter-church relations, the emergence of Evangelicalism, evangelization, and Christian responsibility toward modern moral issues." His assessment was homey but guarded: "We had a spiritual time. He is so down-to-earth and human, I almost forgot he was the pope." Billy wouldn't have had these kinds of experiences if he didn't learn from his mistakes.

Fertilizer for Success

In his book *Failing Forward*, leadership expert John Maxwell writes, "Most people try to avoid failure like the plague. They're afraid of it. But it takes adversity to create success."[xliv] Rick Pitino, one of the most successful college basketball coaches of all time, argues that failure is just "fertilizer" for future success. "The only time failure is truly bad," he writes, "is if you use it as an excuse to quit."[xlv]

Billy experienced failure very early in his ministry—his first sermon, for instance, delivered while he was a college student in Florida. David Aikman explains what happened at a small Baptist church in northeast Florida:

> Prepared with notes for four sermons, Billy was so rattled by his first experience of public speaking to complete strangers that he rushed through all his notes in a single eight-minute

sprint. He was mortified by the experience, but [the school's academic dean, Rev. John Minder] had plenty of faith in Billy and arranged other opportunities for him to preach.[xlvi]

As his influence expanded, his mistakes did more damage. During Billy's visit to South Africa in 1973, he gave an unguarded comment that shot him in the foot. Since the U.S. Supreme Court had recently handed down the *Roe v. Wade* decision, upholding the legality of abortion, a reporter asked Billy if he considered abortion the taking of human life. Billy said yes, he did, but that such a procedure might be justified in certain situations, such as pregnancy caused by rape.

Billy's unfortunate tendency to allow a key word or image to send his mind down a "rabbit trail" then led him to make an unprompted comment about a newspaper article he had read the day before about the gang rape of a twelve-year-old girl. He said he advocated strict punishment for rape, and then added, "I think when a person is found guilty of rape, he should be castrated. That would stop him pretty quick."

Billy immediately knew that he had gone too far, saying, "It was an offhand, hasty, spontaneous remark that I regretted almost as soon as I said it." South African papers paid it little attention, but in America it created uproar. Yet he quickly put out this media fire by admitting he had spoken unwisely. His previous failures prepared him for handling this debacle, which he dealt with gracefully by offering a formal apology.

The Safety-First Mindset
Failure often prevents leaders from taking risks, but giving in to fears stunts leadership gains. Billy refused to live with a safety-first mindset.

When he decided to go to Russia against the advice of the State Department and many high officials, as well as some of his own advisers, he suffered the impact of the fallout. Ultimately, he was vindicated, but not every risky venture turns out that way.

Billy was intent on avoiding all unnecessary or foolish risks, as we see with his "Modesto Manifesto," and his constant weighing-in-the-balances of options and appearances. But he was also always taking risks. Every time he appeared on television, held a press conference with reporters who could blindside him, or traveled in troubled countries, he opened himself to all sorts of consequences. Taking risks day after day, year after year, will open the door to the possibility of failure.

At the 1951 Fort Worth crusade the Graham team made a risky decision: They launched their first feature-length film. The film, *Mr. Texas*, told the story of a rodeo rider who came to know Christ at a Graham crusade. In what Billy later called "a fit of brashness," they rented the Hollywood Bowl for the world premiere of the film. They invited some of Hollywood's best-known film executives and hired twenty-five searchlights to crisscross the sky. The entire premiere nearly came crashing down when the sound and projector malfunctioned. Billy reflected, "I wanted the earth to open up and swallow me, I was so embarrassed!" He also added, "As I look back, I blush at our brazenness—not just in that lighting effort but in the whole project—and at the extent to which our youthful zeal sometimes outraced our knowledge."[xlvii] One filmmaker told Billy, "It's not technically a good film, but the message comes across."

But despite all the problems with the film, it was definitely worth the risk. When Billy gave the invitation at the end of the film, 500 people in attendance at the Hollywood Bowl responded. In the ensuing years, *Mr. Texas* was shown in many parts of the world, and Billy continually met people who came to Christ as a result of seeing the film.

The Beauty of Grace

Failures range from honest mistakes to sinful choices. Throughout his entire career, Billy was brutally honest about the corrupting power of sin. In a 2013 interview in *Christianity Today*, Billy said:

> In the 21st-century society, people have given sin a makeover, calling sin a mistake. God calls it iniquity. It is a disease of the soul. Society generally wants to campaign against disease, raise money to eradicate it. But the disease of sin is celebrated and glorified by society and especially in the pop culture of the day, ignoring the toll it takes in the physical, emotional, and spiritual realms. Society may boast that "sin is in," but the truth is that sin is in you, me, and everyone.

For Billy this wasn't depressing because it awakens us to our deepest need—salvation in Christ. In many ways, this was the grand theme of Billy's entire life. Toward the end of his autobiography, Billy reached out and shared what he considered the amazing good news of admitting our sin and receiving Christ's forgiveness:

> God has done everything possible to reconcile us to himself. He did this in a way that staggers out imagination. In God's plan, Jesus paid the penalty for our sins, taking the judgment of God that we deserve upon himself when He died on the cross. ... God has done everything possible to provide salvation. But we must reach out in faith and accept it.[xlviii]

For Billy, this wasn't merely correct doctrine, it was the way he lived his whole life. Understanding this message of grace and forgiveness makes it easy to admit mistakes and even blatant sinfulness.

Redemptive Failures

Billy's authentic experience of God's grace allowed him to display radical grace to others who needed to "reach out in faith and accept it." His relationship with singer-songwriter Johnny Cash serves as a profound example of this dynamic. Throughout Cash's incredible nearly fifty-year career that ended when he died from diabetes complications in 2003, Cash struggled to live out his Christian faith. His life was fraught with what he called "goof-ups." In an interview with *Rolling Stone*, Cash elaborated on these:

> I used drugs to escape, and they worked pretty well when I was younger. But they devastated me physically and emotionally—and spiritually... [they put me] in such a low state that I couldn't communicate with God. There's no lonelier place to be. I was separated from God, and I wasn't even trying to call on him. I knew that there was no line of communication. But he came back. And I came back.[xlix]

When he slipped back into amphetamine usage, he could get out of control. Cash also felt let down by some of the ministries that he had latched onto for help. Johnny Cash biographer Steve Turner said that Cash felt that "some failed him, some exploited him." But throughout many years of addiction and spiritual darkness, Graham remained a faithful friend to Cash. Cash gravitated toward Graham's consistent display of integrity and openness.

Turner wrote, "Billy was a beacon to Cash who didn't change. Billy remained a stable character."

When Cash fell off the wagon, he likely didn't confide that to Graham, though June Carter Cash may well have shared it with Ruth. The two wives constantly prayed with each other for their husbands and children. Whether Graham knew about all the details of Cash's "goof-ups," his response to Cash was as a loving friend, loyal through thick and thin. "Daddy stayed his friend, that's all," said Franklin. In the 1980s, there was a tabloid uproar over claims that Cash was having an affair and was too stoned to appear at two Graham crusades. Cash denied the drug usage and said no one could separate him and June, although Cash later checked into a drug rehabilitation program.

Billy continued to invite Cash to his crusades and encourage Cash after he got clean from drugs to finally finish his book on the apostle Paul, *Man in White,* in 1986. On the event of Cash's death, Billy Graham said, "Johnny Cash was not only a legend, but was a close personal friend. Johnny was a good man who also struggled with many challenges in life."

Failure Can Make or Break Us

Failure can either break us with shame and defensiveness, or it can remake us with wisdom and humility. Billy allowed failure to make him wise. Toward the end of his autobiography, Billy candidly admitted, "I have much to be grateful for as I look back over my life, I also have many regrets. I have failed many times and I would do many things differently."[1] Then he proceeded to list those things he would like to have done differently. It's a poignant reflection from a man who could have focused solely on his accomplishments and let his failures slide by.

After analyzing great individuals who shaped the twentieth century, Graham biographer David Aikman said, "Virtue, after all, often consists not so much in the absence of fault altogether as in the speed and grace with which fault is recognized and corrected."[li] Billy certainly wasn't without fault, but he did quickly recognize and learn from his mistakes. That is the path of true wisdom for any leader.

PART FIVE
FAITH

In one sense, everything Billy Graham did as a leader flowed from his faith. How he shaped his character, chose his mission, formed his team, and dealt with challenges could all be traced to the same source—his faith in Christ. As Billy said, "Being a Christian is more than just an instantaneous conversion; it is like a daily process whereby you grow to be more and more like Christ."[lii] In other words, Billy truly believed and practiced the New Testament admonition to grow and keep growing in the grace and knowledge of Jesus Christ (see 2 Peter 3:18).

This section focuses on three ways that Billy's faith continually deepened in the grace and knowledge of Christ. Chapter 12 explores the humble openness that made Billy a lifelong learner on the Christian journey. More than anything else, this mindset spurred him to keep practicing the spiritual disciplines that move us forward in faith. Chapter 13 focuses on one specific aspect of his spiritual growth—his commitment to pray on a consistent basis. Chapter 14 concludes the book by emphasizing the key attribute undergirding Billy's entire approach to leadership—love. Of course, for Billy, love wasn't just a vague concept. Instead, for Billy, love always implied a love shaped by the God of love, the love that God demonstrated most clearly through the sacrifice of his Son, Jesus Christ.

CHAPTER 12
BECOMING A LIFELONG
LEARNER

According to surgeon and essayist Dr. Atul Gawande, doctors perfect their surgical techniques the same way other people learn to play the oboe, hit a perfect tennis serve, master chess, or fix a hard drive—by practicing. "There have been many studies of elite performers," Gawande observes, "and the biggest difference researchers find between them and lesser performers is the cumulative amount of deliberate practice they've had." Like these "elite performers" from other disciplines, surgeons must also learn by an ongoing commitment to practice their craft. "I am in my seventh year of [medical] training," Gawande writes. "Only now has a simple slice through skin begun to seem like nothing, the mere start of a case.... I am, I found, neither gifted or maladroit. With practice and more practice, I get the hang of it."[liii] For a medical doctor practice shouldn't stop at the end of residence. Effective doctors understand that the process of learning is a lifelong commitment.

In a similar way, Billy Graham understood that the Christian life also involves a lifelong commitment to keep growing in Christlikeness. Discipleship—the decision to follow Jesus Christ and become his apprentice—isn't a one-time decision. Christians are people who continually practice becoming like Christ. Very early in his Christian life, Billy decided to become a learner. In so many words, like Gawande, Graham conveyed a similar approach to the Christian life: "With practice and more practice, I get the hang of it."

John Akers contends that Billy's lifelong commitment to practice certain spiritual disciplines was at the foundation of his ministry success. Akers called it Graham's "deeply felt commitment to a consistent, thoughtful devotional life." Without this deeply felt commitment to keep growing in Christ, Akers argues, "Graham never would have become the person he was, nor would he have had the worldwide impact he did." But Graham's ability to remain a lifelong learner on the path of following Jesus "kept him humble, reinforced his integrity, expanded his vision, and enabled him to keep his focus."

Rain for Our Roots

In one sense, there was nothing unusual about how Billy Graham approached his practice of following Christ. For his devotional life, he kept up a daily practice of reading and meditating on the Bible. He also maintained a consistent time of prayer (the focus of the next chapter). Like millions of other Christians, he had learned early in his life the practice of setting aside a definite time each day to be alone with God. According to Akers, this was "a practice he sought to maintain even in the midst of overwhelming pressures, disruptions, and frequent travel."

In Graham's article titled "The Book that Gives Life," he writes, "Through my years of experience I have learned that it is far better to miss breakfast than to forgo a session with God's Word. It's not that Bible reading is some kind of religious fetish bringing good fortune, but that I lack the decisiveness and purpose and guidance when I neglect what is more important than the food that is necessary for my body."

So Billy set aside time every morning to read and meditate on a few chapters of Scripture. But this wasn't a perfunctory religious duty. His time in Scripture often involved a deeply personal encounter with the Living God who addressed Billy through his Word. "Sometimes the Word makes such an impact on me," he claimed, "that I have to put the Bible down and get up and walk around for a few moments to catch my breath.... If I ever get to the place where the Bible becomes to me a book without meaning, without power, and without the ability to rebuke my own heart, then my ministry will be over, for the Bible has been far more than my necessary food."

Graham didn't restrict this spiritual practice to just a set time in the morning. Even in personal conversation or ministry team meetings, he frequently opened his Bible or spent time reflecting on what God was teaching him. As he stressed in his 2011 book *Nearing Home*, "The Bible is the constant rain that waters our root system of faith. It is the inspiration from which we drink daily."[liv]

Lessons on an Old Crate

The people who knew Billy best all say that Billy also made a lifelong practice of learning from other people—and not just the powerful and well educated. He went out of his way to receive important lessons about following Christ from the quiet and humble.

In a conversation with Billy's brother Melvin about the powerful Christian leaders who influenced Billy, Melvin told the story about one of Billy's important "mentors"—an unassuming workingman named Bill Henderson. Melvin described Henderson as a "tiny fella" who had a little grocery store in the African American section of Charlotte. Henderson had long sleeves that came way down, and he wore a tie that would hang down below his waist. "But I tell you," Melvin said, "that little old man, he knew the

Bible!" Bill Henderson loved God, and he knew how to put his faith into practice.

By the late 1940s, Billy had already traveled and preached throughout Europe, but whenever he returned to Charlotte, he liked to visit Bill Henderson. Melvin said, "In the afternoons Billy would go there and just sit and talk to him. He'd sit on an old crate—I don't think they had a chair in the place—and let Bill Henderson teach him."

Melvin's image typifies Billy's lifelong practice of learning from almost anyone. Fresh from air travel all over the world to address large audiences, Billy took time to sit on a crate so a humble, ordinary shopkeeper could teach him about the Bible and following Jesus. Billy himself said of his early ministry, "Learning was an insatiable desire with me. I burned to learn, and I felt my limitations of schooling and background so terribly that I determined to do all I could through conversations, picking up everything I could from everybody."

A Ripple Moving Outward

The picture of Billy sitting on an old crate and listening to Bill Henderson blends with his lifelong practice of finding and learning from seasoned mentors. He carefully studied the company of evangelists who preceded him, people like Dwight Moody, Charles Finney, and Billy Sunday. He gathered all sorts of publicity, church mobilization, and programming ideas from the game plans of Moody and Sunday. Billy was always quick to learn from anyone with a better idea or a better method.

He especially resonated with current leaders who had deep faith and a sharp intellect. And when those two traits came in the same package, the attraction was almost irresistible. In Oxford in 1947, Edwin Orr was writing his doctoral dissertation on the Second

Great Awakening. In that academic atmosphere, he and Billy talked of Wesley and Whitefield and the marks of true revival, praying together for another Great Awakening.

Billy was also ready to learn from intellectuals who differed from him. He never flinched at connecting with scholars but positioned himself as a learner with deep appreciation for scholarship and its role—and yet he was also clear about the limits of the intellect.

Billy listened to those close to him, including, perhaps first of all, his intelligent and perceptive wife. Ruth was crucial to Billy's success, and her advice often influenced his decisions. In the 1950s, for instance, when she heard that Billy had speculated he might be elected president if he ran on the right platform, Ruth called him and, with her typical dry and trenchant wit, said she didn't think the American people would vote for a divorced president, and if he left the ministry, he would certainly have a divorce on his hands. When it came to Ruth, Billy almost always got the point—and quickly, too.

William Martin claimed that listening to others was one of Billy's great strengths. "He never hardened into the place where he assumed, 'Here I am. I'm Billy Graham, and you and your ideas can bounce up against me.' No, he was always willing to grow, like a ripple that is constantly moving outward in an ever-growing circle. He showed that in his willingness to cooperate with more and more different groups."

The Long Obedience

Although Billy listened to a wide array of sources, ultimately he developed a lifelong practice of listening to and then obeying God's voice. In this regard, he practiced what pastor and author Eugene Peterson called "a long obedience in the same direction."[lv] Billy's long and dedicated obedience was practiced in countless small and quiet ways, but on at least one occasion, his obedience was forged in the crucible of a relational crisis.

This particular crisis was precipitated by his early colleague, Chuck Templeton. They had ministered together in Youth for Christ, and Billy had considered Chuck more gifted in many ways than he. Templeton went on to Princeton Seminary, where he began to doubt significant tenets of the faith. Billy would meet with him in New York, where Templeton would pose questions about the Bible and theology that Billy could not answer. It became a painful crucible, and Billy understood the stakes. If he had significant doubts about the Scriptures and felt he was being intellectually dishonest, he would lose the call and the power that fueled his ministry. It rocked him to the core.

Through discussions with both Templeton and biblical scholars and colleagues, and through long and agonizing periods of reflection and prayer, he broke through to a certitude that he could rely on the Scriptures and the essentials of Christian faith. Billy had carefully weighed all the contrasting input from others, mixing it with prayers and tears and laying it all before God. As those who knew Billy have said, in times of great challenges, he would call on the Lord with great fervor. Allan Emery, a longtime Graham friend and BGEA board member, observed that the difference he saw in Billy—contrasted with so many other leaders—was that when confronted with a crisis, he would spend literally an entire night in prayer seeking God's direction and empowerment.

Although the Templeton experience forced Graham to drive stakes into the ground that would anchor his ministry, issues of strategy presented different sorts of crucibles. He would have to weigh advice against advice, friend against friend, faction against faction. For example, when he had to decide whether or not to go to the Soviet Union in 1982, the pressure was intense. Likewise, passionate calls for him to start a Christian university were so strong that he purchased land in North Carolina and began the process, and then eventually backed off. Years later, proponents of the university concept were still deeply disappointed.

While these decisions tore Billy in two directions, he maintained a remarkable ability to listen to others but then stay rooted in God's will. Some would say Billy listened to too many people and wrestled with decisions too long and made too many U-turns. But the bottom line was that he wrestled and prayed them through until he felt confident about God's will. As Jay Kesler said, "The great issue of our day for leaders is how to lead in a postmodern, pluralistic, multicultural environment. How does one maintain convictions with civility? Billy Graham has done that. This is to me the largest leadership quality needed in the modern world."

The Power in Weakness

Billy Graham had an amazing ability to learn from almost anything in life—even his own weaknesses. Joni Eareckson Tada offers one of the most poignant stories about this aspect of his leadership. In one sense, Joni is an expert on learning from weakness. As a teenager, a diving accident left her paralyzed from the neck down. Naturally, at first the accident was devastating. She nearly gave up on God. Through the years Joni's faith eventually blossomed and she even went on to found Joni and Friends, an organization that encourages and equips those with disabilities. But all of this happened in the midst of Joni's great weakness.

Joni shared the following story about her experience at Billy's Moscow crusade in the early 1990s:

My translator was Oleg, a young Russian man who was severely visually impaired. He commented while we were on the platform, "Joni, isn't it wonderful that God is using me, a blind boy, and you, a paralyzed woman to reach the people in my nation of eleven time zones?" I got a lump in my throat, just thinking of his point: that God delights in choosing weak people to accomplish his work. I was about to respond to Oleg when I saw Billy Graham slowly rise (with a little help) from his seat to walk to the platform. It was around the time he had received an initial diagnosis of perhaps Parkinson's disease. As I watched Mr. Graham steady himself to step up to the pulpit, I said to Oleg, "Friend, God is using not only a blind boy and a paralyzed woman but an elderly man on shaky legs to reach your people!"

How did Billy react when she shared those thoughts with him? Joni said, "He wasn't embarrassed. This is what has inspired me most about this extraordinary leader. Not only does he keep moving ahead, despite his physical challenges, he seems to boast in them." Then she pointed to 2 Corinthians 12:9—"My grace is sufficient for you, for my power is made perfect in weakness." Joni continued:

Mr. Graham is keenly aware that God's power always shows up best in weakness. This is why he inspires me with my own disability of thirty-seven years. His example of perseverance under pressure speaks volumes to me and to many others. It's probably why the BGEA, with every crusade, systematically in the spirit of Luke 14:21 "goes out into the streets and alleys" to "bring in the poor, the crippled, the blind and the lame." This tells me Mr. Graham knows God's heart when it comes to the lowly and needy. He reflects this through his own humility, and he lives it daily.

The Mark of a Great Soul

Journalist David Aikman includes Billy Graham as one of six "great souls who changed the century." He writes that Billy made mistakes of judgment at different points in his career, but he "never stopped admitting his own faults and weaknesses." Billy's greatness of soul flowed from his lifelong practice of learning from others and growing in Christ. Aikman put it this way: "To remain humble, teachable, and gracious amid success and in the face of sometimes bitter opposition and criticism is the mark of true virtue. And to remain relentlessly loyal to God's call while exposed as consistently as Graham has been to all the world's power and glory, well, 'tis the mark of a Great Soul."

But Billy summed up best when he said—well into his eighties at this point—"I am a man still in process." That sentence sums up his practice of living as a lifelong learner.

CHAPTER 13
GROWING IN PRAYER

In his book *Nearing Home*, Billy wrote that he often got letters from older people who seem to lament, "All I can do is pray." Billy says that he'll write back and say, "God bless you for doing the most important thing."[lvi]

For Billy, prayer really was "the most important thing." He knew that nothing of significant or eternal value could be accomplished apart from prayer—just as you can't accomplish anything with a power tool apart from plugging it into an adequate power source. Sadly, in the midst of pursuing good and worthy goals, many men and women involved in Christian leadership have neglected the source of spiritual power.

Russ Busby, one of the Graham organization's first employees, pointed to one primary thing behind Billy's success: his ability to plug into God, the true power source. Busby said, "He listens for what God says to him; so when Billy says something, it comes out of his own experience. … His ideas are uncanny. God has given him the most unusual vision in almost every area of sharing the Good News. It has to be a gift from God!"

That doesn't imply that prayer always came easy for Billy. He was open about his own struggles. At one point Billy talked about a time when he prayed "long and earnestly" when he was going through a dark period, but there was no answer. He said, "I felt as though God was indifferent, and that I was all alone with my problem. It was what some would call 'a dark night of the soul.'" In this case, Billy shared his feelings with his mother, who urged him to "reach up by faith in the fog and you will find his hand will be there." He took her advice and "experienced an overwhelming sense of God's presence."

And yet, this experience didn't lead to a permanent spiritual victory. Instead, on a regular basis Billy had to plug into the Source of power in the midst of human frailty and imperfection. "Every time I give an invitation, I am in an attitude of prayer," he said. "I feel emotionally, physically, and spiritually drained. It becomes a spiritual battle of such proportions that sometimes I feel faint. There is an inward groaning and agonizing in prayer that I cannot possibly put into words."

So over and over again Billy returned to the practice of genuine and passionate prayer. A deeply felt sense of his own inadequacy drove him to his knees, causing him to plug into the prayers that provided the power for his half-century ministry.

The "First Rule" of Prayer

Catholic philosopher Peter Kreeft once wrote: "The first rule for prayer, the most important first step, is not about *how* to do it, but to *just do it*; not to perfect and complete it but to begin it. Once the car is moving, it's easy to steer it in the right direction, but it's much harder to start it up when it's stalled."[lvii]

From the beginnings of his ministry, Billy practiced Kreeft's "first rule for prayer." Billy's colleague, T.W. Wilson, called him "the most completely disciplined person I have ever known." The discipline started around 7 A.M. each day, when he would read five psalms and one chapter of Proverbs. He started there because, as he often said, the Book of Psalms showed him how to relate to God, while Proverbs taught him how to relate to people. After breakfast he would pray and study more Scripture. Even under the pressure of travel schedules, moving from city to city and hotel to hotel, often through many time zones, he strove to study and pray each morning. Billy knew he could nothing without prayer, nothing in his own power.

Billy's prayer connection was not only unusually fervent, it was also as natural to him as breathing. Billy knew he needed to pray continuously in order to draw the strength he needed. Larry Ross told the story of his initial discovery of Billy's incessant prayer connection:

> The very first time I set up a network interview for Mr. Graham was with NBC's *Today* show in 1982. I went in the day before to meet with the producers and ensure everything was set. I assumed Mr. Graham would want to have a time of prayer before he went on national television, so I secured a private room. After we arrived at the studio the following morning, I pulled T. W. Wilson aside and said, "Just so you know, I have a room down the hall where we can go to have a word of prayer before he goes on TV."
>
> T. W. smiled at me and said, "You know, Larry, Mr. Graham started praying when he got up this morning, he prayed while he was eating his breakfast, he prayed on the way over here in the car they sent for us, and he'll probably be praying all through the interview. Let's just say that Mr. Graham likes to stay 'prayed up' all the time." We didn't need to use that room. That was a great lesson for me to learn as a young man.

Pressures into Prayer

Billy Graham's colleagues often spoke of the constant pressure Billy felt during his ministry. Imagine the pressure of conducting the funeral for the disgraced former President Richard Nixon while the nation skeptically watched and listened for every nuance. Imagine the emotional demands on him when he conducted the memorial service after the Oklahoma City bombing. Imagine the service at the National Cathedral right after the 9/11 attacks on the World Trade Center and the Pentagon. The nation was in deep shock, and the entire world was watching on TV. Billy's words and tone, both for Americans and for people of all other nations, had to be just right. That would be challenging enough even at the height of one's powers. Billy was frail and in his eighties, with serious health problems, yet he mounted the platform with steadiness and told the nation, "God is our refuge and strength; an ever present help in trouble. Therefore we will not fear, though the earth give way, and the mountains fall into the heart of the sea." Despite his frailty, Billy's presence, poise, and message touched the sorrows and fears and brought hope and a deeply Christian response to his nation and to the world. He found the inner resources to rise to that momentous occasion.

By the time Billy was in his sixties, it seemed reasonable that he should retire from all the pressure of carrying the weight of his organization. Many assumed that, with all the health problems Billy was already experiencing, he would change his pace, step down from his leadership role, and get out of the spotlight's glare. Instead, he continued holding meetings all over the world for another quarter century. He continued to stay in the trenches and lead his organization. He continued to appear on news shows to represent the gospel. He made countless public appearances while keeping up private connections with close colleagues. He also continued to minister to every U.S. president of his era and participate in their inaugurations. In the phrase voiced by President George W. Bush when Billy was hospitalized and unable to attend the funeral of Ronald Reagan, Billy was "the nation's pastor"—but he was also the leader of an organization and of a vast movement.

How could he maintain the strength and sense of commitment to do all that, not only in his last decades but throughout the unrelenting pressure of the leadership sprint-marathon he ran for sixty years? Billy turned these high-pressure events into an opportunity for prayer.

The foundation for this intensity in prayer was laid in Billy's life well before his public evangelistic ministry. For example, William Martin tells the story from Roy Gustafson, one of Billy's groomsmen and a close colleague. Roy, Billy, and two other men were walking out in the hills, talking about an important decision. They agreed to pray. Billy said, "Let's get down on our knees."

Roy was wearing his only good suit, so he got his handkerchief out, laid it down carefully, and knelt on it. As they prayed, Billy's voice sounded muffled to him. Roy opened his eyes and saw that while three of them were gingerly kneeling, Billy was flung out prostrate on the ground, praying fervently, oblivious to the dirt.

This readiness to fling himself into prayer in the midst of pressures continued to mark Billy's approach to life and ministry. In his October 1956 New York crusade, for example, Billy candidly wrote in his journal, "There are many friends who have predicted that the New York Crusade could end in failure. From the human viewpoint and human evaluation it may be a flop." And yet Billy was able to cling to prayer as the only way to surrender these fears. He continued, "I am convinced in answer to the prayers of millions that in the sight of God and by heaven's evaluation it will be no failure. God will have his way. I have prayed more over this assignment and wept more over the city of New York than any other city we have ever been to. Now it is in God's hands."

Deep Wrestling

Even in the early days of youthful vigor, the demands on Billy made him intensely aware of his need for that power. When the 1957 New York campaign was so effective that the pastors asked him to stay for another month of meetings, he told Grady Wilson he didn't think he could make it even one more day. "All of my strength has departed from me. I've preached all the material I can lay my hands on. Yet God wants me here." In all, he wound up preaching virtually every night there for over three months, making additional public appearances and speaking at many of them during the day.

Grady Wilson believed it was "the prayers of people all over the world" that gave Billy the needed stamina for the task. Yet he also believed that the grueling time in New York drew down his reserves. "Since that time, I don't believe he's ever regained all his strength."

Cliff Barrows agreed. "Bill was so weary in the latter few weeks, he felt he just couldn't go another day, but the Lord kept giving him strength. But at the end of the meetings, something left him, something came out of him physically that has never been replaced."

Despite the recurring sense of being drained and empty, Billy didn't quit. As Grady observed, "When he mounts the platform, though, it seems the Holy Spirit gives him a resurgence of vitality and power."

This is the picture so often described by his colleagues: weakness drawing on the Spirit. And it wasn't simply physical fatigue but a wrestling with the realities of the human condition and his own shortcomings. "All of us are awfully human," observed Grady. "Billy is painfully aware of his humanity. He has a temper, but he keeps it in check." How? "He stays close to his Lord and spiritual discipline and prayer."

Rick Marshall, in his first meeting with Billy, was amazed at his being so open about his fatigue and by his humble prayers.

I remember thinking to myself, *This is Billy Graham?* It was such a contrast to the persona I had watched filling the stadium with his booming voice and authority. But when I was actually with the man, I was overwhelmed by the humility, the raw honesty before God about his own inability and physical limitations. That was the way I viewed him for the next twenty-three years. It kept me willing to stay within an organization that placed a lot of demands on me.

Rick quoted the apostle Paul's statement, "When I am weak, then I am strong," as setting the basis for this strange mixture of strength through weakness. Like Paul, Billy leaned into his weaknesses.

"Now think about it," Rick said. "If anyone could have been confident, it would have been Billy. But I never saw that. I saw only humility and a bowed head. In fact, I made it a point for the last twenty campaigns to bring a team of pastors to pray with him every night before he went into the pulpit. That, I think, became for him one of the most important moments. It was his way, too, of saying, 'I don't do this in my own strength.'"

Through Not *From* Him

Because Billy realized the power didn't come *from* him but *through* him, he didn't feel obligated to overreach with his methods. Jack Hayford, himself a powerful preacher, observed:

Billy Graham reveals a remarkable absence of the superficial, of hype, or of pandering to the crowd.... His communication consistently avoided exaggeration or "slick" remarks. There's never been anything cutesy or clever about his style. There are no grandiose claims or stunts employed to attract attention. Graham merely bows in prayer while seekers come forward— moved by God, not a manipulative appeal.

That confidence in the power of the prayer frees the leader from having to work overly hard on presentation techniques designed to convince the hearers.

During the 1956 meetings in India, Billy was thrust into a position where he had to grab onto the power of prayer and hang on with radical intensity. In the city of Palamcottah, an estimated crowd of 100,000 attendees threatened to turn the evangelistic meeting into a riot. Graham later wrote, "I bowed my head and prayed a prayer I have not prayed for a long time. It was almost a prayer of commanding, a prayer of authority. I remember I opened my hand as though to come down upon the crowd, and I said, 'Oh God, stop the noise; quiet the people now.'"

Billy said that as "deathlike hush" came over the crowd, he preached for over an hour with a feeling of "tremendous power and liberty." Then, he reports, "Pentecost fell." After nearly 4,000 people streamed forward to receive Christ, the team had to stop the invitation because there was no more room up front. In his room that evening, Graham wrote, "Certainly tonight's demonstration of the Spirit is the deepest and greatest I have ever sensed."[lviii]

Truly, it was an incredible demonstration of the power of God released through prayer.

A Way of Life

It wasn't enough for Billy to develop his personal prayer life. He also wanted to inspire and challenge other leaders to plug into the true power source. Bob Cooley talked about Billy's influence on him in this regard. Billy, as a founder of Gordon-Conwell Seminary, spoke at Bob's inauguration as its president. He said:

> I remember his admonitions to me. In the casual conversations that surrounded that event, he emphasized strongly the importance of a life of prayer and spiritual formation in leading the seminary. He kept saying, "I know how much you're going to have to depend upon this." That struck me right at the beginning, because coming out of the university, I didn't have anyone who would take that message to me. But he kept emphasizing this.

Bob then talked about how that had played out during his many years as the seminary's leader.

> I immediately established the discipline of daily prayer in the president's office. I invited everyone and anyone who would join me for prayer. My day began with prayer. I had one professor, J. Christy Wilson, who never missed a day during his time at the seminary in joining me. It was the discipline of committing to prayer, sharing needs, concerns, and praise. Those were essential disciplines that I tried to not just model but to make integral to my daily life.

These were types of disciplines that Billy implemented in his own leadership. He constantly surrounded himself with friends and pastors who would pray with him and for him. Just as these voltage-producing friendships strengthened Billy in his preaching, so it empowered Bob Cooley's leadership. "It did in a number of ways," Bob said. "It created more joy within. You can easily get entrapped in the wake of the day's programs and concerns leading an organization—no wonder the word *burden* comes to mind. The weight of the issues can rob you of your joy. But prayer teaches you that rejoicing becomes an activity. It's more than a feeling. It's a discipline. It's a daily thing."

The Power Unleashed

One thing is certain about Billy's life: He believed in the power that God unleashes through the ordinary prayers of ordinary Christians. In 2003, Billy wrote, "From one end of the Bible to the other, we find the record of people whose prayers have been answered, people who turned the tide of history by prayer, men and women who prayed fervently and whom God answered."[lix]

On another occasion Billy added, "Tennyson's well-known words, 'More things are wrought by prayer than this world dreams of,' are no mere cliché. They state a sober truth." Billy believed and personified that, and it made possible his ability to lead others in those great endeavors.

CHAPTER 14
LEADING WITH LOVE

John Corts, a key employee of the Graham organization for thirty-five years, ten of them as its president, was once asked, "What would you say is the bottom line distinctive of Billy's leadership?" After a long pause, John said emphatically, "Love. The difference between him and so many other leaders is that whatever the circumstances, Billy always led with love."

Numerous leaders in Graham's organization have confirmed John's assertion: Billy led with love.

Yet some would ask: What does love have to do with leadership? Aren't the essential requirements of leadership to be results-oriented and to personify authenticity and employ a variety of techniques and emphases? Not according to Hudson Armerding, former president of Wheaton College. In his book on leadership, he says, "When the characteristics of leaders are enumerated, love is not usually included. Yet this quality is central."[lx] Or as Martin Luther King Jr. once said, "Whom you would change, you must first love."

Somehow, in the most difficult situations, Billy communicated a heart full of love for others. People sensed it. His love deepened through the years as he listened intently to the Spirit, whose first fruit the Bible says is love.

The Foundation of Love
Billy's decision to build his ministry and message on love started early. He did not react in kind to the bitter criticisms of those

fundamentalists who were outraged by his having Catholics and "liberals" on his platform. He responded with silence and with love.

At the founding of *Christianity Today*, surveying the personal attacks and divisiveness among conservative Christians, he wrote that the magazine should set as its goal "to lead and love rather than vilify, criticize, and beat. Fundamentalism has failed miserably with the big stick approach; now it is time to take the big love approach."

In answering his critics, Billy said in a very early issue of *CT*, "The one badge of Christian discipleship is not orthodoxy but love." Editor of *Christianity Today* Carl Henry said much the same thing, criticizing not the theology of fundamentalism but its "harsh temperament" and its "spirit of lovelessness and strife."

Billy's friend Francis Schaeffer would later expand on this in his book *The Mark of the Christian*. In it, Schaeffer asserts that the authentic work of a follower of Jesus is love. He quotes the "last commands" of Jesus to his followers as he was about to leave them: "I will be with you only a little longer. A new commandment I give you: love one another. As I have loved you, so you must love one another."

Billy took this command from his Leader very seriously. To many ears, the fact that Billy would call employees like Sherwood Wirt "beloved" sounds strangely foreign. But the word not only comes from the Bible, it was what Billy felt toward his fellow disciples and what he determined to make central in his life.

The love Billy talked about wasn't just a vague, unspecified love. His entire concept of love flowed from the biblical story of God's love for lost sinners, especially the love of Christ that was revealed at the cross. In 1960, in an article titled "What Ten Years Have Taught Me," Billy stressed that he centered his message on the cross of Christ and its dual message of the "sins of men" and the "unwearying love of God." Four years later, he offered the following summation of his message: "I stress a great deal the love of God from the cross saying to the whole world, 'I love you, I love you, I will forgive you.'"

It's a fascinating footnote that Mordecai Ham, the hard-nosed fundamentalist at whose meetings Billy was converted, later noted with remorse that he wished he could restart his ministry and "love people" as Billy did. Perhaps Mordecai, who was known for his anti-Catholic, anti-Semitic statements, got the message too late, but Billy's example shaped thousands of leaders in orthodox Christian activism, helping them build their ministries on the love of Christ.

The Need for Love

Billy believed education and legislation were important but inadequate. In light of the world's atrocities, he wrote in *The Secret of Happiness*:

> Government and civil laws are like the cages in a zoo—they can restrain evil, but they cannot change the basic nature of the human heart. Art and education may refine the taste, but they cannot purify the heart. The Holocaust was carried out by educated people, some brilliantly so.

When he and Ruth visited the Nazi death camp of Auschwitz, they were deeply moved.

> We saw the barbed wire, the instruments of torture, the airless punishment cells, the gas chambers and crematorium. Every square foot of that terrible place was a stark and vivid witness to man's inhumanity to man. We laid a memorial wreath and then knelt to pray at a wall in the midst of the camp where 20,000 people had been shot. When I got up and turned around to say a few remarks to those who had gathered with us,

my eyes blurred with tears and I almost could not speak. How could such a terrible thing happen—planned and carried out by people who were often highly educated?

Billy's commitment to love and mercy clashed prodigiously with obvious evil. "I would rather have a world filled with ignorant savages," he said, "than with civilized sophisticates without morality."

When John Akers was asked how Billy's visits to Auschwitz, Treblinka, and refugee settlements in India fit with his intense focus on his mission, Akers said:

Simply this—he's a compassionate person. In regard to the Holocaust, he was very aware of the history of Christians persecuting the Jews. He wanted to identify with their suffering, their moral outrage, and to agree that this must never be allowed to happen again. That's part of his moral leadership.

The Width and Breadth of Love

Two years after 9/11 with its destruction of the World Trade Center, Billy was holding meetings in Dallas. Some Americans felt all Muslims were suspect. Billy's colleague, Rick Marshall, said:

It surprised me to learn that one of the largest U.S. populations of Muslims is in central Texas. We were at Texas Stadium in October, right between Dallas and Fort Worth. Billy did an interview with *The Dallas Morning News*, and one of the questions the writer put to him was, "Dr. Graham, do you have a message for the Muslims of Texas?" He answered without hesitation.

The next day the headline on the front page, bottom section was "Billy Graham has a message for Muslims: 'God loves them, and I love them.'" It was a powerful statement. Talk about cutting right to the heart of the gospel! Everyone was talking about it, because it defused so much anger and so much criticism. It brought to the table the hallmark of Billy's ministry.

When asked how Billy preferred to handle religious and other differences, Rick said, "Billy has always been theologically rooted in grace. The imperative for him was evangelism—the evangelist sees the heart. If it's Muslims, or Hindus, or anyone else, his focus is to love them and to share with them the love of Christ."

His emphasis on love spanned the entire spectrum of cultural divisions. Homosexuality, for instance, has wrenchingly divided both culture and the church. As with his stance toward other religions, Billy has clear theological parameters. But his message to gays and lesbians was not laced with judgments.

When Hugh Downs interviewed him on the 20/20 television program, the subject turned to homosexuality. Hugh looked directly at Billy and asked, "If you had a homosexual child, would you love him?"

Billy didn't miss a beat. He answered gently, "Why, I would love that one even more."

The emphasis on love does not brush away the terrible realities of Muslim-Christian conflict, or the tensions stirred by polar-opposite beliefs about homosexual behavior, or other chasms on important issues of our day. Billy was painfully aware of them. He realized that people will have their differences and not every dispute can be resolved.

No Little People

Francis Schaeffer liked to say, "There are no little people; there are no little places." Schaeffer added that all truly great Christian leaders have a gentleness and tenderness that is manifested in the way they gladly expend time and energy on "little people," the people that may not seem significant in terms of the leader's "big agenda." Billy shared Schaeffer's "no little people, no little places" motto.

For example, one day during a break at a Christianity Today board meeting, Billy and some other trustees stepped into a hotel hallway. Far down the dim corridor was a cleaning lady who looked toward them and smiled. Then she motioned with her hand a timid hello.

Billy broke from the other trustees and walked down the hall to talk to her. She had watched him on television, she had been to one of his crusades, and she had appreciated his ministry. Billy graciously talked to her for several minutes before rejoining the group, but both the woman and the trustees were impacted by his simple action of breaking from the press of issues and reaching out in simple, gracious friendship.

Gerald S. Strober, author of *The Day in the Life of Billy Graham*, shares another story about Billy's compassion for an alleged "little person" named Rivka Alexandrovich, a Soviet Jewish woman from the city of Riga. Here's how Strober told the story:

> She came to the United States to attempt to win public support for her daughter, Ruth, then a prisoner of conscience in Russia. I called Billy one afternoon and reached him in the barbershop of Washington's Madison Hotel. After hearing of Mrs. Alexandrovich's problem, Billy invited me to bring her to Chicago in two days' time so he could meet and talk with her. The Chicago session was packed with emotion. There was definite positive chemistry alive in the room, and Billy expressed great sympathy for young Ruth Alexandrovich. At one point in the conversation, he walked to the telephone, took out an address book, and dialed a long-distance number.

"Is Henry there?" he asked. "Well, tell him to call me the minute he comes in."

No one in the room had to ask who "Henry" was, and there was little doubt in our minds that the call had been placed to Key Biscayne, Florida, where Henry was staying with his boss, the president of the United States.

Five minutes later the telephone rang, and it was Henry [Kissinger]. Graham gave him a briefing on Mrs. Alexandrovich (he had carefully jotted down the pertinent facts as she talked), and he then asked the caller to try to do something for the distraught émigré. Later that night, Graham issued a statement from his Minneapolis headquarters calling attention to the plight of the Soviet Jews. Two months after the Chicago meeting, Ruth Alexandrovich landed at Lod Airport in Tel Aviv.

Frank Thielman, whose father was Billy and Ruth's pastor in Montreat, has shared stories of Billy's generosity, including handing over their house keys. "When my dad was sick and in need of rest," Frank explained, "the Grahams sensed his need. They were going away for three weeks, and they told my mom and dad to just come up there and stay at their house. So our family did that for three weeks. That's amazing—it's a real example to me." Frank also mentioned how the Grahams often helped the destitute. "Montreat is in the rural southern Appalachian mountains," he said. "They would unhesitatingly give and help the poor. They are very generous people."

Billy also described his own awakening to the needs of the Appalachian core.

One Christmas Eve a friend came to my house and said, "Would you like to go out with me distributing Christmas packages up in the mountains?" I was glad to go. And I was in for one of the greatest surprises of my life! I thought everybody in our community had all the necessities of life. But I was taken back into some little mountain valleys where people did not have enough to wear, enough to eat, and could not even afford soap to wash their bodies. Appalled and humbled, I asked God to forgive me for neglecting the people in my own community.

Fierce Love

Yet for all Billy's kindness and compassion, his love also had a tough side. At times, he was confronted with situations requiring more than compassion. As C.S. Lewis observed, "Love is something more stern and splendid than mere kindness."

John Akers said that although Billy could usually disarm hostile situations, sometimes he was forced to be stern. "He was in Communist East Germany to speak to a Lutheran synod," John told us. "The reception was so cold, the conveners so arrogant, that when he got up he said, 'When I came in, I had seldom met such a hostile group, and it shouldn't be that way. We are brothers in Christ, and I love you. But this atmosphere does not reflect that.'"

John remembers that Billy's forthright statements "just wiped them out." They got the message—sometimes "tough love" requires redemptive correction.

Former President George Bush also experienced Billy's fierce love. In the summer of 1985, then Vice President George H.W. Bush invited Billy to their family home in Maine. The senior Mr. Bush gathered his children around the fireplace to discuss "spiritual issues" with Billy. At the time, the younger George Bush was struggling with a drinking problem. During the conversation Billy turned to the younger Bush and asked directly, "Are you right with God?"

"No," Bush replied, "but I want to be."

Billy's display of "something more stern and splendid than mere kindness" sparked a change in the heart of the future president. "He didn't lecture or admonish," Bush said. "Billy Graham didn't make you feel guilty; he made you feel loved." And yet at the same time, Bush felt the heat in Graham's fierce love. Bush added, "Over the course of that weekend, Billy Graham planted a mustard seed in my soul, a seed that grew over the next year. He led me to the path, and I began walking. I had always been a religious person, had regularly attended church, but that weekend my faith took on a new meaning... where I would commit my heart to Jesus Christ."

Such is the power of fierce love.

The Power of Presence

Sometimes love is shown by a thoughtful word, by a willingness to help an employee in trouble, or by a refusal to retaliate when attacked; other times love is shown by simply showing up.

At the time Billy was in his mid-eighties and struggling physically, Leighton and Jean Ford's daughter, Debbie—Billy's niece—had successfully endured cancer treatments but then learned the cancer had recurred. Debbie was apprehensive as she entered the Mayo Clinic in Jacksonville, Florida, for a bone scan.

I was very fearful of cancer being found somewhere else in my body," Debbie said. As she walked back to her room, she glanced down the empty hallway. There at the end, sitting in a wheelchair and facing her direction, was a frail, older man. She realized it was Billy, who happened to be at Mayo for some tests.

Knowing I was there, he had asked the Mayo staff to locate where I was in the clinic. I ran and threw my arms around him and sobbed with all my heart. He held me tenderly, saying over and over, "I love you."

When I looked up to tell him how frightened I was about my recurrence, I saw that he was also crying. In his own weakened state, he met me at my weakness.

Debbie was deeply touched by this evidence of Billy's love for her.

Then Debbie offered a fitting summary to the Billy Graham, the man who built his life on, preached on, and shared with others the love of Christ.

"Certainly he's a great evangelist and confidant of leaders," said Debbie. "He's also a tender and frail older man. Despite the fact that he hurts like I do and has concerns for his body like I do, he's thoughtful and caring and willing to take time for me, just as I am."

Leading with love—that was the essence of Billy Graham's leadership genius. When we consider his fierce and tender love for teammates and critics, hotel employees and future presidential candidates, Muslims and Soviet Jews, destitute Appalachians and sick relatives, it's easy to understand how essential love was to his leadership—and his entire mission.

ENDNOTES

i   William Martin, *A Prophet with Honor* (New York: William Morrow and Company, 1991), 604.

ii   Patrick Lencioni, *Silos, Politics, and Turf Wars* (Hoboken, NJ, Jossey-Bass, 2006).

iii   Billy Graham, *Just As I Am* (New York: HarperOne, 2007), 243–244.

iv   Nik Wallenda with David Ritz, *Balance* (Nashville: Faith Words, 2013), 207.

v   David Aikman, *Billy Graham* (Nashville: Thomas Nelson, 2007), 294–295.

vi   William Martin, *A Prophet with Honor* (New York: William and Morrow and Company, Inc., 1991), 451.

vii   C.S. Lewis, *Mere Christianity* (San Francisco: Harper San Francisco, 2009), 128.

viii   Alison Beard, "Life's Work: Maya Angelou," *Harvard Business Review,* May 2013.

ix   William Martin, *A Prophet with Honor* (New York: William Morrow and Company, 1991), 545.

x   Sherwood Elliot Wirt, *Billy* (Wheaton, IL: Crossway Books, 1997), 31.

xi   Billy Graham, "A Time for Moral Courage," *Reader's Digest* (July 1964); Reprinted in *The Virgin Island Daily News,* October 29, 1964.

xii   Alan Siegel and Irene Etzkorn, "When Simplicity Is the Solution," *The Wall Street Journal,* March 29, 2013.

xiii   James M. Kouzes and Barry Z. Posner, "To Lead, Create a Shared Vision," *Harvard Business Review* (January 2009).

xiv   Peter Drucker, *The Effective Executive* (New York: Harper Collins, 2002), 112.

xv   John Maxwell, *Sometimes You Win, Sometimes You Lose* (New York: Center Street, 2013).

xvi   Drucker, ibid, 107.

xvii Jim Collins, *Good to Great* (New York: HarperBusiness, 2001), 59.

xviii *Charles Moore, Daniel H. Burnham: Planner of Cities* (Boston: Houghton Mifflin Company, 1921), 147.

xix   Kevin McCoy, "Survey Finds Wall Street Ethics in Decline," *USA TODAY,* July, 17, 2013.

xx   Harold Myra, "Billy Graham's Fiscal Leadership," *Outcomes,* Summer 2009, http://ym.christianleadershipalliance.org /?page=billygrahamleader, last accessed on October 8, 2013.

xxi   Billy Graham, *Just As I Am* (HarperOne: New York, 2007), 185.

xxii Quoted on *Beliefnet,* "Billy Graham Organization Is Exemplary, Charity Organizations Say," http://www.beliefnet.com /News/2002/10/Billy-Graham-Organization-Is-Exemplary -Charity-Auditors-Say.aspx, last accessed on October 8, 2013.

xxiii Ibid.

xxiv Graham, op. cit., 439.

xxv Billy Graham, *Ask Billy Graham* (Thomas Nelson: Nashville, 2007), 101.

xxvi John C. Maxwell, *Teamwork 101* (Nashville: Thomas Nelson, 2009), 9.

xxvii   Jonah Lehrer, *Imagine: How Creativity Works* (New York: Houghton Mifflin Harcourt, 2012), 144–152.

xxviii   Billy Graham, *Just As I Am* (New York: HarperOne, 1997), 663.

xxix   Jim Collins, "The Wizard, the King, and Hobbit of Business," *Fast Company*, April 2004.

xxx   John Tierney, "24 Miles, 4 Minutes and 834 M.P.H., All in One Jump," *The New York Times*, October 14, 2012.

xxxi   John Ortberg, *If You Want to Walk on Water You've Got to Get Out of the Boat* (Grand Rapids, MI: Zondervan, 2001), 47.

xxxii   John Ortberg, "Don't Waste a Crisis," *Leadership Journal*, Winter 2011.

xxxiii   The Editorial Board, "Lincoln at Gettysburg Long Ago," *The New York Times*, November 17, 2013.

xxxiv   Adam Richter, "Six facts … about the Gettysburg Address," *Reading Eagle*, November 19, 2013.

xxxv   Billy Graham, *Just As I Am*, 258.

xxxvi   Mary Karr, interview, quoted in Wesley Hill, Writing in the Dust blog, February, 26, 2012.

xxxvii   William Martin, *A Prophet with Honor* (New York: William Morrow and Company, Inc., 1991), 74–75.

xxxviii Billy Graham, *Hope for the Troubled Heart* (New York: Bantam, 1993), 84.

xxxix   Billy Graham, *The Journey: Living by Faith in Uncertain Times* (Nashville: Thomas Nelson, 2007).

xl   R.O. Blechman, *Dear James: Letters to a Young Illustrator* (New York: Simon and Schuster, 2009), 30–34.

xli   Steven Snyder, *Leadership and the Art of the Struggle* (San Francisco: Berrett-Koehler Publishers, 2013), 3–7.

xlii   Martin Zeilling, "If You Haven't Failed, Then Maybe You Aren't a Real Entrepreneur," *Business Insider*, October 25, 2013.

xliii   J.K. Rowling, "The Fringe Benefits of Failure, and the Importance of Imagination," *Harvard Magazine*, June 5, 2008.

xliv   John Maxwell, *Failing Forward* (Nashville: Thomas Nelson, 2007), 15.

xlv   Rick Pitino, *Success Is a Choice* (New York: Crown Business, 1998), 209.

xlvi   David Aikman, *Billy Graham* (Nashville: Thomas Nelson, 2007), 40.

xlvii   Billy Graham, *Just As I Am*, (San Francisco: HarperOne, 1997), 175–176.

xlviii   Ibid., 728.

xlix   Anthony DeCurtis, "Johnny Cash Won't Back Down," *Rolling Stone*, October 26, 2000.

l   Billy Graham, *Just As I Am*, 724.

li   David Aikman, *Great Souls* (Lanham, MD: Lexington Books, 2003), XIV.

lii   Franklin Graham and Donna Lee Toney, *Billy Graham in Quotes* (Nashville: Thomas Nelson, 2011), 84.

liii   Atul Gawande, *Complications* (New York: Picador, 2003), 15–22.

liv   Billy Graham, *Nearing Home* (Nashville: Thomas Nelson, 2011), 153.

lv   Eugene Peterson, *A Long Obedience in the Same Direction* (Downers Grove, IL: IVP Books, 2000), 5–10.

lvi   Billy Graham, *Nearing Home* (Nashville: Thomas Nelson, 2011), 157.

lvii   Peter Kreeft, "Time," PeterKreeft.com, accessed October 31, 2013, http://www.peterkreeft.com/topics/time.htm.

lviii William Martin, *A Prophet with Honor* (New York: William Morrow and Company, Inc., 1991), 194–195.

lix Billy Graham, compiled by Bill Adler, *Ask Billy Graham* (Nashville: Thomas Nelson, 2007), 138.

lx Hudson T. Armerding, *The Heart of Godly Leadership* (Wheaton, IL: Crossway Books, 1992), 65.

ABOUT THE EDITOR

Matt Woodley is the managing editor for PreachingToday.com, a ministry of *Christianity Today*. After pastoring three churches for over twenty years, Matt currently serves part-time as the Pastor of Compassion Ministries at Church of the Resurrection in Wheaton, Illinois. He has authored four books, including *God with Us: The Gospel of Matthew* and *The Folly of Prayer*. He has also contributed numerous articles to various publications, including *Leadership Journal*, *In Touch* magazine, and *Neues Leben*.

Since 1956, *Christianity Today* has challenged the church with real-world content that is timely, compelling, insightful, balanced, and biblical. *Christianity Today* publishes a multitude of resources, in various formats, that Christian leaders everywhere trust.